# UNCONSCIOUS PUTTING

# UNCONSCIOUS PUTTING

---

Dave Stockton's Guide to
Unlocking Your Signature Stroke

**DAVE STOCKTON**
with Matthew Rudy

GOTHAM BOOKS

GOTHAM BOOKS
Published by Penguin Group (USA) Inc.
375 Hudson Street, New York, New York 10014, U.S.A.
Penguin Group (Canada), 90 Eglinton Avenue East, Suite 700, Toronto, Ontario M4P 2Y3, Canada
(a division of Pearson Penguin Canada Inc.); Penguin Books Ltd, 80 Strand, London WC2R 0RL,
England; Penguin Ireland, 25 St Stephen's Green, Dublin 2, Ireland (a division of Penguin Books
Ltd); Penguin Group (Australia), 250 Camberwell Road, Camberwell, Victoria 3124, Australia
(a division of Pearson Australia Group Pty Ltd); Penguin Books India Pvt Ltd, 11 Community
Centre, Panchsheel Park, New Delhi—110 017, India; Penguin Group (NZ), 67 Apollo Drive,
Rosedale, Auckland 0632, New Zealand (a division of Pearson New Zealand Ltd); Penguin Books
(South Africa) (Pty) Ltd, 24 Sturdee Avenue, Rosebank, Johannesburg 2196, South Africa

Penguin Books Ltd, Registered Offices: 80 Strand, London WC2R 0RL, England

Published by Gotham Books, a member of Penguin Group (USA) Inc.

First printing, September 2011
10  9  8  7

Copyright © 2011 by Dave Stockton
All rights reserved

Gotham Books and the skyscraper logo are trademarks of Penguin Group (USA) Inc.

LIBRARY OF CONGRESS CATALOGING-IN-PUBLICATION DATA
has been applied for.

ISBN 978-1-592-40660-9

All photos courtesy of J. D. Cuban

Printed in the United States of America
Set in Berkeley Oldstyle
Designed by Julie Schroeder

# CONTENTS

Foreword by Phil Mickelson      vii

Preface by Dave Stockton Jr. and Ron Stockton      ix

Introduction      xi

*Chapters*

*One*      Your Putting Signature      1

*Two*      Create a Picture      11

*Three*      Let It Go      23

*Four*      Roll Your Ball      35

*Five*      Why You Three-Putt      53

*Six*      The Mental Game      61

*Seven*      Why Equipment Matters, and When It Doesn't      69

*Eight*      Troubleshooting      77

Acknowledgments      91

# FOREWORD

## by Phil Mickelson

For a number of years, I had been putting very sporadically, and I really didn't have any direction. I didn't know what I was trying to do with my putting. I was getting frustrated, so asked my caddie, Bones Mackay, who I should go see, and he recommended Dave Stockton.

I had obviously heard good things about the work Dave had been doing with other players, but I was looking forward to hearing his assessment of my putting game. We met in San Diego in September 2009, at The Bridges, and spent two days having breakfast and then putting for a couple of hours. I knew this was going to be a good fit immediately. He's so positive and so much fun to be around, and I had instant respect for him—the career he has had and the major championships he's won give him a lot of credibility.

As we started working, I knew it was going to end up going well, because he made putting simple for me again. With Dave, putting started to feel like it did when I was a kid. As a professional, I had started to overcomplicate things, and knowing the importance of making putts, I got caught up in results. I started focusing too much on mechanics and technique, and I stopped seeing the line as well.

Dave simplified all that, quickly.

I started to look at the hole and the line of the putt longer, and by taking the back of my hand and making it the putterface, I don't even need to look at the alignment of the putter anymore. I'm just taking the back of my hand at the hole, which really simplifies the process. I feel like I'm putting with direction—whether I have a good putting day or not. I feel like I'm getting back into the feel of the putt—trying to make a good roll—and not getting caught up in the mechanics. I'm seeing the line again, and I'm feeling really good over the ball.

After those couple of days with Dave, it didn't take long to start seeing more putts go in. I had 36 one-putts at the Tour Championship the next week. Up to that point in the 2009 season, I had made thirteen putts of more than 20 feet all year. At East Lake, I made nine in four rounds and won the tournament. When you can focus on a simple, concise routine and you're seeing the line well, the confidence that follows is extremely valuable—especially at a place like Augusta National.

I'm grateful for Dave's help, and I'm sure you'll enjoy putting a lot more after you hear what he has to say.

Phil Mickelson
May 6, 2011

# PREFACE

*By Dave Stockton Jr. and Ron Stockton*

The lessons, strategies, and philosophies you're going to read about here in *Unconscious Putting* are special ones to us. We've been sharing them week in and week out in clinics full of 20-handicappers and in consultation with the best players in the world on every major professional tour.

But it's more than that.

The ideas in this book are the same ones we grew up with. As kids, we learned to see the line and follow a routine listening to Dad—and to our grandfather, Gail—and that teaching style never changed. He's always talked about feel, and the importance of using your imagination to create a shot in your mind before you hit it. The ideas are simple, and they've been tested and perfected through more than seventy years of competition, from our grandfather's time learning from Alex Morrison and playing with greats like Walter Hagen to Dad's time on the PGA and Champions tours, to our experience of playing on teaching on the professional tours.

They're part of our family tradition.

That family element is also what has made the last couple of years so satisfying. Working together in the "family business" has been fantastic, and we're looking forward to helping a lot more people in the years to come. We all have our strong opinions, but when it comes to instruction, we're all in agreement. And the players we've helped—from 90-shooters in a clinic in Colorado to a multiple major-championship winner like Phil Mickelson—have gotten the benefit of that insight and experience.

We've heard some people say you can't reach everyone. That some teaching philosophies just don't work for some players. In the decades of teaching and playing experience we have as a group, we don't think that's true. We've all worked with players who came away from a lesson feeling like they didn't get what they were looking for.

But that's almost always because of the dominant culture in golf instruction these days—the cult of "mechanics." A lot of players think that if they aren't overhauling the way they hold it or the way they stroke it, they aren't going to get better. You can even see the disappointment flicker on their faces when we tell them there's no golden mechanical piece to the stroke that will solve every problem.

Our hope is to show all the players we teach in a lesson, clinic—or through this book—that it is simple, but that it doesn't come from mechanics. The mind controls what you do on the putting green. Stay open to that fact and learn to embrace your own personal putting signature and how to see the line and you can dramatically improve how you roll your ball—with the stroke you have. Even the tour players we teach will often finish a first lesson making a bunch more putts and tell us that it has to be tougher than this. That putting can't be that easy. It's so satisfying to spend some time with a player like Martin Laird—who was ranked near the bottom in the tour putting stats—and see him gain confidence almost immediately and pour a putt right in the heart to win a huge tournament like Bay Hill. And Martin was just one of more than two dozen tour players—Justin Rose, Yani Tseng, Morgan Pressel, Adam Scott, Michelle Wie, Massy Kuramoto, Matt Kuchar, Sean O'Hair, Suzann Pettersen, and J. B. Holmes are some others— who understood the value of better putting and dramatically improved after coming for help.

We've seen it over and over again, in just a thirty- or forty-five-minute lesson. Read the book and give it a chance, and you'll see it for yourself.

# INTRODUCTION

How much of this game is mental?

If you walk the golf instruction aisle at the bookstore, subscribe to one of the popular golf magazines, or listen to some instructors teach, you could get the idea that how you hold the club or how well you copy a series of positions determines whether or not you can play golf. The mental side might get some attention here or there, but it's seen as a kind of "accessory" to the real meat and potatoes—swing mechanics.

To me, that's backward.

Are mechanics a part of the game? Absolutely. You make the physical job of hitting a shot easier the closer you get to "standard" when it comes to setup and the swing. But putting is a completely different animal. Even on the longest putt, the putterhead moves a couple of feet at most. Success is determined by how well you sort out the speed and break of your putt and translate that read into the roll of the ball. By how well you use your head—and then get out of your own way emotionally.

Putting is an art. But a vast majority of teachers treat it almost the same way they do the full swing—with a series of diagrams and technical advice about the shape of the stroke and the percentage of weight that should be distributed on each foot, or with some kind of training aid.

In *Unconscious Putting*, I'm going to introduce you to an easier, more instinctive way to putt. Instead of being locked up thinking about your stroke or trying to copy positions, you'll be locked in—on the line and on rolling your ball.

How do I know it's easier and more effective? I've won twenty-five times on the PGA and Champions tours—including two PGA Championships on the regular tour and three majors as a senior—on the strength of my putting. I was never a long hitter, and I was never even in the top half of all ballstrikers on tour. I made my money hitting eight or nine greens and taking twenty-five or twenty-six putts, using the same approach I learned from my father sixty years ago.

And it's something that can be taught. To anyone.

The proof is out on tour today. Between me and my sons, Ron and Dave Jr., we worked with players who won twenty-nine times on the professional tours in 2010—from Phil Mickelson at the Masters to Yani Tseng at the Nabisco and Women's British Open. And the lessons are about as far away from a swing teardown as you can get. A player will call one of us to schedule a day, and I've yet to give a lesson that takes more than four hours—and that includes both putting and chipping.

I've done thousands of corporate outings in the last forty years, and my experience with average players has been the same. Giving a 15-handicapper some advice about grip or stance is nice, but it pales in comparison to showing them how to actually see the line and roll a putt while that line is still fresh in their subconscious mind.

And that's what we're really shooting for here—to show you how to engage your mind productively and efficiently in all the steps leading up to the putt, and then how to turn it off and let the unconscious mind take over.

You can change the way you putt. You can feel like you have a legitimate chance to make every one you look at, no matter if you've made the last five or missed them. Here's the blueprint for how we'll get there.

In Chapter One, I'm going to explain the concept of a putting signature. It's simple, really. In the course of your day, you perform lots of activities while on autopilot—you aren't giving any conscious thought to making the motions that make up the activities. When you drive your car, you don't think specifically about every little movement you have to make to get the car to turn and stop. Writing your signature is the same way. When you sign a check, you grab a pen and just do it, with no extra attention paid to how you make the lines. Good putters handle this part of the game in the same way. Instead of consciously attempting to replicate a specific series of movements, the stroke is in the background.

Chapter Two covers where that focus *should* be—on the path of the putt to the hole. Many players don't understand how to read a putt to determine speed and break. If you don't have a good feel for break and speed, you're not going to have an accurate mental picture of the ball rolling along the right line and falling in. And that's what separates the best putters from the rest—the ability to see that line.

Once you see the line, how do you make the ball go where you intend? The key is to stop cluttering your pre-putt routine with steps that at best don't do anything to help you roll the ball on line, and at worst, actively hurt your chances to do it. In Chapter Three, we'll talk about a simple pre-putt routine that will keep you focused on your line and set up in a way that makes it shockingly easy to get the ball rolling where you want it to go. And you'll do it without a practice stroke.

Stroke mechanics are far down on my list of things that need tinkering in most players' putting games. If your mind is right, you're going to make more than your share of putts. But having a handle on a few basics—setup and stroke fundamentals tuned for your body type and putting style—will help you diagnose and correct your own putting game when you struggle. I'll explain some ways to use your putter more efficiently in Chapter Four—and how to roll your ball, not hit it.

In Chapter Five, we'll talk about why you three-putt. Judging speed and break poorly is just the start. If you aren't approaching your longer putts with the same sense of strategy that you would for a tee shot on a tricky par-5 with trouble on both sides, you're selling yourself short. You'll learn how to leave yourself in easier positions to tap in when you have something left to clean up.

More than any other factor, the quality of your self-confidence—and your self-talk—determines the quality of your putting skill. In Chapter Six, we'll talk about the importance of believing you can make any putt you see—even after you've had a bad couple of holes—and how you can build that confidence.

Chapter Seven covers the tool you have in your hand. We'll talk about selecting the right putter for your style and your eye, and how lie, loft, length, and optics impact its performance. We'll also cover some of the truths and myths about putters—which "rules" about grip size, grip material, weighting, and head shape are good to follow and which you can ignore. And in the last section, Chapter Eight, we'll go over some simple troubleshooting tips you can use to sort out the problems you might encounter out on the course. I'll also talk about some of the lessons and drills that the boys and I have used to help players like Phil Mickelson, Adam Scott, Matt Kuchar, Massy Kuramoto, Martin Laird, J. B. Holmes, Suzann Pettersen, Annika Sorenstam, Yani Tseng, Sandra Gal, and Morgan Pressel on professional tours around the world.

You'll find that the ideas here are a little different than the ones you might have come across in other instruction books and articles. I'm sure it will feel a little strange the first time you go out and actually play a round where you get into your putting stance while looking at the hole—and going straight into your putt without taking a practice stroke.

But trust me—and trust the power of your unconscious mind—and let the results speak for themselves.

# UNCONSCIOUS
# PUTTING

# ONE

# Your Putting Signature

If you come and see me for a lesson, the beginning of it is going to look very similar no matter if you're a 15-handicapper doing a three-day golf school or a Masters-winning tour player looking for an edge.

It's going to start with a simple piece of paper and a pen.

I'll ask you to sit and sign your name, just as you would if you were signing a check.

How much thought did you put into your signature?

There's no right or wrong answer. Some people use the pen like a paintbrush and make an elaborate, careful signature. Most people just write it out without even a conscious thought. They've been doing it for so long that it's second nature.

Once you've signed your name on the piece of paper, I'll ask you to do one more thing: Go back and try to copy the same signature right below it, slowly. It's really difficult to make an exact duplicate when you're doing it consciously, isn't it?

The point I'm trying to illustrate with this little exercise is that it's always much easier to perform a physical move that is locked comfortably into your subconscious mind than it is to make a very specific *effort* to do the same move.

Let me give you another example.

I live about seventy-five miles inland from the Southern California coast. If I get in my car to drive over to the beach, I'm rolling down the window, resting my elbow on the windowsill, and holding onto the steering wheel while I listen to the radio and enjoy the drive. I've been driving for more than fifty years, and I'm way past the point where I have to consciously think about how and when to accelerate or brake or turn. The act of driving is embedded in my subconscious mind.

Put yourself in that same scenario. You're driving home on a route you've traveled a million times before. What happens when a police car pulls out and starts trailing you?

All of a sudden, all those movements that used to be embedded in your subconscious move to the forefront, into the conscious mind. You're thinking about how fast you're going. You're worrying about the cop's assessment of your driving, and whether or not you might get pulled over. In other words, it's taking an extreme amount of additional energy and attention to do something that you previously hadn't even given a conscious thought to.

The unfortunate reality is that this is how most people putt as if they were getting tailed by somebody about to give them a ticket. They play nervously, trying to replicate a stroke rather than *make* a stroke.

To me, that's no way to play. And it doesn't have to be for you, either.

The overwhelming majority of the teaching that my sons and I have been doing over the last few years has shown players how to unlock the natural, free-flowing, athletic stroke they have inside them.

We've been teaching average players and tour players alike the art of Unconscious Putting.

There's really no trick to it. At its core, Unconscious Putting involves learning how to accurately see the optimum line that a putt should take to the hole and giving yourself a consistent pre-putt routine that lets you preserve that visualization and roll the ball on your intended line.

The problem with a lot of putting instruction out there—whether it's from teachers, in books, or in magazines—is that it places a tremendous emphasis on copying and repeating a mechanically "sound" stroke. I'm not criticizing the intent behind all of that. When you learn how to drive a car, you do have to learn how to hold the steering wheel, use the gas, and follow traffic rules.

But the two main problems I have with this emphasis on mechanics are that it leaves out the most important part of putting—the mental side—and it encourages you to trace somebody else's signature instead of signing your own. When you're concentrating so hard on what your hands are doing, how far to take back the putter, whether it's going back in a straight line or on a slight arc—or any other bit of mechanical information—you're diverting your attention from where it should be: on line and speed.

I'll tell you some things right up front that will probably be very different from any other putting lesson you've had. It doesn't really matter to me if you have a short, quick stroke or a long, flowing one. You don't have to have a stance that's perfectly square to the target line, or a ball position that stays absolutely locked in day in and day out.

What you do need to have is a setup and a stroke that suits you—your temperament, your body type, and what makes you comfortable. We're all built differently. If you're a tall person with long arms, you're going to feel better in a different stance than a shorter, rounder person with shorter arms. If you have a thick and muscular but less flexible upper body, you're going to power your swing—and your putting stroke—differently than a thinner, more flexible person.

People obviously have different temperaments, too. You might walk, talk, and move fast. A high-energy person is going to naturally have a different putting stroke than a slower, more deliberate person. We process information differently, too. The way you process information might be different from mine. Some people thrive on a visual confirmation from a caddie or a partner of the line they see, while other players see what they see and want to be locked in on just that, without any other opinion distracting them.

On top of all that, a person just doesn't feel the same from day to day. People aren't machines. Some days, it might feel better to have a little wider stance and a ball position a little farther forward. I encourage every player I teach to be receptive to those feelings, and to go with them. I get asked all the time about my ball position, or exactly how wide or open my stance is when I putt. The answer—"It depends . . ."—must be frustrating for people who want exact measurements, but it's true.

The lesson I'm trying to give here is the one my dad, Gail Stockton, gave me more than fifty years ago. The best putters are players who spend almost all of their energy and focus on the line and speed of the putt, and almost none of it on mechanics. They connect with the "feel," not with a mechanical checklist of body parts and movements.

As I said before, mechanics *do* play a role, especially if you're a beginner or a player who can't make the most basic repeatable contact with the middle of the putterface. Developing some solid basics—which we'll talk about a little bit in Chapter Four—is like going to driver's training class as a fifteen-year-old. You learn how to start the car, put it in gear, hold the steering wheel, accelerate, turn, and stop. Once you know those things, then you learn how to *drive*. Real driving is diagnosing the situations that unfold in front of you and responding to them with physical movements that are virtually subconscious. Watch a NASCAR driver make a pass at 200 miles per hour and try to tell me that he's thinking about how far to move his hand on the gear-shift lever, or how many inches he should adjust the wheel to the left. He isn't. Those movements have been shifted to the background. The same has always been true for me when I'm standing over a putt on the first green (or the 72nd) at a PGA Tour or Champions Tour event. When I'm going through my routine, I'm determining my line and the speed I want to roll the ball, and narrowing my mental focus—which we'll talk about more in Chapter Three. I don't think about the mechanical process of rolling the ball any more than I'd think about the mechanics of dropping an ice cube into a glass of water.

By the end of this book, you'll be there too with your putter.

How can I be so sure? Because I'm teaching you to do something you already know how to do. You've just covered it up with a lot of extra bits and parts that make putting way, way more complicated than it needs to be. We're going to go back to how a kid learns to putt.

My dad was the first professional at Arrowhead Country Club in San Bernardino, California. I grew up three houses down from the golf shop, and from the time I was three, I was out at the course messing around with my 3-wood, 8-iron, and putter in a little bag.

I don't remember too many long-game lessons he gave me in the beginning—or very many of the short-game ones, either—but looking back, it's amazing how well he prepared me for a career as a tour player and eventually as a teacher.

Ninety percent of what he gave me consisted of mental fundamentals—how to visualize a putt or a shot. The rest was a series of subtle tips on fundamentals and advice about equipment. His knack was taking each individual and helping them feel comfortable. When I was a kid, he'd give me something about my grip to work on, then let me go out and hit shots and play the game.

I'd take the tip and work on it for a few hours, then go back to him and tell him I got it, and that I was ready for the next one. He would brush me off and tell me to just go play. He never told me why we were working on this or that, and it would actually sometimes make me mad and think that he didn't care. But it was the opposite. He knew the value of implanting something in my subconscious and letting me go and establish it completely before introducing something else.

My dad also understood the value of keeping me hungry for the game. When I was fifteen, I had a pretty serious surfing accident. I was in shallow water getting ready to paddle out when a girl near me lost control of her board—one of the big, heavy, wooden nine-footers we used back then. The board shot up and cracked me in the back, knocking me silly. I was pretty shaken up, but after some time on shore I got back in the water and finished up the day surfing. The pain in my back just wouldn't go away, however, and I finally went to the doctor. He said I had six cracked ribs. The injury pretty much ended my baseball and basketball careers (such as they were). I knew that if I wanted to get a scholarship to go to college—and that was going to be the only way I could afford to go—golf was going to have to be my vehicle.

I played for the school team that next season, but my dad had arranged for me to go work for a friend of his at the Gibson lumberyard, like I had since I was thirteen. I don't think I played more than four rounds of golf from June to September. When I got back to school in the fall, all the guys I had beaten the previous spring were better than me, and I had to work to catch up. My dad wanted me to keep that thirst to play, and to inspire my competitiveness.

I ended up getting a scholarship to play at the University of Southern California—the same school where my dad was an All-American player in the 1930s. The golf coach at USC then, Stan Wood, had no idea what he was getting with me. My competitive history had really only started when I was seventeen. My dad had loosened his restrictions a little and I was allowed to play four tournaments. One was the national Hearst tournament, sponsored by the newspaper chain. In the regional qualifying tournament at Riviera, I made a 10 on the first hole after hitting it in the barranca, and seventeen holes later I shot 75 and qualified for the match-play portion. Once I got there, nobody took me past fifteen holes, and the next thing I knew, I was headed for Albany, New York.

Traveling across the country was a big deal for me—the only place I had ever been before then was to see my grandparents in Tucson. I ended up finishing second in the national tournament, so I got to go down to New York City for the awards presentation. I went and saw the Empire State Building and the Statue of Liberty. Later that same summer, I played in the U.S. Junior and got to the quarterfinals. Those two tournaments got me scholarship offers from two schools—USC and Arizona. I picked USC because I could move away from home and still come home for weekends.

When I got to Los Angeles, I joined the Kappa Alpha fraternity. Right up there on the wall in the frat house was a picture of Al Geiberger—"The Human 1-Iron." He had just left a legacy of fifty-three straight team match wins at USC for the PGA Tour, and he was my idol.

In those days, there was no fall golf, and you couldn't play as a freshman. Spring came around, and Coach Wood asked me if I'd drive a car down to Tucson for a quad match against UCLA, Arizona, and Arizona State. Once we got down there, I went out and played with the coaches while the matches were going on. I shot 66—and the best score to count for USC that day was 74. Geiberger's streak was done, and it was a long spring waiting for my chance to play.

By my junior year, I knew I wanted to play professional golf, but my dad wanted to make sure I had a backup plan in place. My dad had been a golf pro, and a great player. I have a picture of him with Walter Hagen before an exhibition they played in the 1930s. But even good players didn't always have a way to make steady money in the 1930s (or even the 1960s), so my dad moved on to teaching, and then to owning his own shop, Stockton Sporting Goods. He wanted me to have a degree to fall back on if I needed it, so I got mine in general management and finance—and even came back for a semester after I finished my senior golf season to clean up my last seven credits.

College golf was all about the team, and the individual scores you shot were secondary to how the Trojans made out. I won a few tournaments here and there—including the Pac-10 individual title, just as my dad had. But playing in the U.S. Amateur in 1963 gave me my first real taste of what it was like to compete on my own ball. I drove with my buddy Roger Cleveland (who ended up building some pretty nice wedges) in his Volkswagen Beetle across the country to Wakonda in Des Moines, Iowa, to play in the amateur. You haven't lived until you pass a truck in a Beetle on a two-lane bridge. The car levitated.

When we got there and saw the draw, Roger had a first-round bye, while I had Bill Hyndman, who had played in everything—North and South, Masters, British Amateur. Meanwhile, my bio was one line—San Bernardino, Calif. I knew Roger was going to be around for at least two days because of that bye, so I was bound and determined to at least get out of the first round so I wouldn't have to wait for him. I beat Hyndman 7 and 6.

A three-putt actually ended up costing me a chance to get into the Masters, back when all four of the semifinalists from the Amateur the previous year were invited. I lost in 21 holes to Walter Stahl in the quarterfinals after three-putting from 20 feet on the 18th. I was pissed off about how I finished, but riding back with Roger (who ended up losing in the third round), I knew I could compete with even the best amateurs—guys like Deane Beman (who had won the tournament) and George Archer.

I just had to go out and prove it.

I met my wife, Cathy, during my senior year at USC while she was living in Redlands, California. Not only was she the California Citrus Queen, but she was my first and only blind date, set up by my mother. We got married on February 27, 1965, after I finished school. My grandmother and two businessmen from San Bernardino, Ken Hunter and Stick Reilly, each put up $2,000 to sponsor me, and I turned pro. Cathy and I packed up our Impala the night of the wedding and we left to follow the tour. We didn't come back until October, because there was no money for us to fly. Cathy's mother would call, and she'd describe some wedding gifts we had gotten so Cathy could send out thank-you notes. We wouldn't see them for months.

Tour golf was a hard road then. I think I spent $7,000 that first year, and made about $5,000. The second year, I spent $8,000 and made about $6,000. But I had a premier case of tunnel vision. I knew I had a great short game—which meant I had half the game licked. I'd call my dad, and I'd describe what kind of shots I was hitting, and he'd help me diagnose my problems. We'd look at my swing on the first, primitive version of video cameras they had in the mid-1960s, and he'd ask me what I saw, and what I needed to do to fix it.

One of the key elements to this on-the-job training I got from my dad was the emphasis on feel and visualization. My dad would never let me hit more than five balls with any one club. If I hit three high hooks, he'd say, hit a low punch shot. I was using my signature, not tracing "ideal" mechanics.

I didn't read a word of any of the golf magazines, or listen to what anybody else had to say about my swing—which wasn't what you would call classic. I think I was a lot like Jim Furyk is today, and the relationship Jim has with his father. Jim doesn't have a conventional swing, but it looks pretty good when he's picking up Player of the Year trophies.

In those first couple of years, I was fortunate enough to have a couple of players take me under their wing and give me some great advice about the mental side of the game—information that just reinforced the lessons I had been getting from my dad for all those years, with the added legitimacy of having been proven out on tour.

I was paired with Don January and Arnold Palmer at the L.A. Open in 1966, my second year, and being under the lights with Arnold was enough to give anybody stage fright. I don't think I'd ever seen as many people in one place at a golf course as there were around the first hole. Don pulled me aside on the first hole, put his arm around me, and gave me some advice about how to play my own game and not let Arnie's Army distract me. Don came from an era when players had to hustle just to make a living. It would have been easy for him to stand back and see if I got buried, but he went out of his way to be incredibly nice.

Al Geiberger went from being my idol at USC to a lifelong friend. He was generous enough to play lots of practice rounds with me when I got out there, and talk to me about all the different courses and the ways he tried to play them. In 1967 at Colonial—a course he had never played very well—he gave me a great plan, and I ended up winning that week. It was my first victory on the PGA Tour.

I would go on to win ten other tournaments on the PGA Tour, including two majors—the 1970 and 1976 PGA Championships. On the Champions Tour, I won fourteen more times, including three majors—the 1992 and 1994 Senior Players Championships and the 1996 Senior U.S. Open.

There are some lessons I learned from those days of tournament golf, and I'm going to share them over the next few chapters. But it was a conversation I had with Byron Nelson in early 1976, at the start of the season when I won my second major, that brought a lot of this into focus for me.

I have always enjoyed hunting and fishing, and that off-season, I went to the Yukon for two weeks. If there was a tag for it, I had it—sheep, mountain goat, bear, moose, elk, you name it. We hiked and hunted and fished and enjoyed the northern lights. It was a fantastic trip.

At the end of the trip, I went directly to Cypress Point for an outing. I didn't even have clubs or shoes—I had to borrow them from Jim Langley, the head professional—who was a good friend from my early tour days. I was standing on the first tee, and I asked myself, *What was I thinking about the last time I hit a ball?* Instead of worrying about it, I just swung the club. I was 7-under through 14 holes, I made a hole-in-one on the 15th and birdied the 16th. I believe I ended up shooting 65.

A few weeks later, I had lunch with Byron Nelson at the Masters. I asked him what he was thinking about in 1945, the year he won all those tournaments in a row. He told me he had one swing thought, and he used it the entire year. He went to the range and loosened up his shoulders, and he went with it.

I started to realize then just what a gift my dad had given me.

At some point, you have to let it go and trust what you know. Your mind pictures yourself doing it, and you do it. The background my dad gave me allowed me to go on tour with that single thought, and forty-six years later, I'm still doing the same thing. I've never heard anything out there that was better than what I had.

Now I'm teaching with my boys, Dave Jr. and Ronnie, and we've talked a lot about my dad's teaching philosophies and have wondered who influenced him. It wasn't until recently that I discovered who it was. Alex Morrison was a prominent teacher in the 1930s and 1940s. He wrote the early instruction book *Better Golf Without Practice,* but is probably most famous for working with Henry Picard. Picard won the Masters in 1938 and the PGA Championship the next year, and went on to help both Ben Hogan and Sam Snead as a teacher. Paging through Morrison's book is like reading a transcript of some of the things my dad told me about the game as I grew up.

Now we're transmitting what my dad knew about this game—and how important the mental side of it is—to the next generation of players. We're bringing the simplicity that Byron Nelson talked about back to the modern player.

It's as easy as signing your name.

# TWO

# Create a Picture

I believe putting is a simple act. You see the line the ball should take to the hole, lock in on that line, and let the stroke go while that line is fresh in your mind.

But for a lot of players, it isn't that simple.

At the start of every lesson I give—to a tour player or an amateur—I ask every player to try the signature exercise we talked about in the last chapter, and then I set up a simple, common situation. I give them a 12-foot putt with about six inches of break, and I say that this putt is to win something important—whether it's a major championship, a card at Q-school, or to win the B-flight of the club championship. I ask them to go through their entire process, from read to actually making the stroke, so I can see how they *see* the putt and how that vision translates into rolling the ball.

Unfortunately, many, many players at every level put up a lot of road-blocks for themselves. They get in the way of their own good putting. They don't get a complete or accurate feel for the line, or they junk up their routine in between the read and the stroke and lose connection with the line they chose—either because they stop actually *looking* at the line, or because they go through an extended set of pre-shot movements that not only disconnect them from seeing the line, but also physically aim them in a different place than they intend.

My goal here is to remind you how simple reading greens—and rolling your ball—really is.

I say "remind" because I really believe that most players already "know" how to do these things. The skills have just been covered up by a lot of unnecessary extras, tics, and habits. Hand a putter to a kid, give him a basic idea of how to hold it, and turn him loose on the practice green. It won't take long for him to intuitively see how the ball reacts to a slope and to start rolling the ball startlingly well. And with no fear. It's only after you increase what you "know"—layers and layers of mechanical advice, "rules of thumb" about green reading, and a fair amount of scar tissue from missing critical putts—that you get away from this natural ability.

Let's talk about seeing the line here.

The whole point of reading a green is to give yourself a mental picture of what the ball will do on the path from where it sits to the hole. You're trying to analyze the conditions—distance, slope, grain—and choose the right line for the situation. You're picking the right combination of pace and direction.

Many players have an elaborate ritual for reading greens that they've picked up piece by piece along the way. Maybe they saw their favorite tour player crouch down behind the hole and focus intently, so they copy that. Or they make an effort to plumb-bob with the putter—even if they aren't quite sure how to do it, or why. After a while, the process turns into a ritual and they go through this elaborate procedure to read the putt, when only some (or none) of the things they do actually give them good information to create that accurate picture of the line. A lot of times, the ritual is really focused on the ball itself, and not where they want the ball to go.

Now, I'm not trying to say that everybody has to have the same green-reading procedure, or that every part of the procedure has to be completely productive. My goal for you is to do what helps you see the line, and what helps you feel comfortable and in a position to trust the line you see and let it go.

The first time I watched Phil Mickelson go through his routine on the 12-footer I described at the beginning of the chapter, I was astonished at his ritual. He basically made a 420-degree circuit around the putt—looking at it from the high side, behind the hole, the low side, behind the ball and back to the apex of the putt's break—all to feel comfortable about the line he was seeing. If all of that helps you see your line, and doesn't get in the way of making a comfortable stroke at a pace that suits you, I'm all for it. But if you have a two-minute reading and pre-putt routine that doesn't help you see the line better or feel more comfortable, all you're doing is giving yourself more time to get nervous and think about the reasons you're going to miss. That's just not productive.

Let me tell you about how I see the line, and maybe it will give you some insight on how to simplify and improve your green-reading process.

First, I believe the art of green reading itself is a dying one, and carts are to blame. When I was a young player, we all walked and carried our own bags. When you approach a green from the front, you can feel the changes in contour and relative firmness of the grass with your feet, and you can see the predominant slopes on the putting surface. You can see which way the green drains—which is also the primary direction putts will break on that hole.

Driving up to the side of the green in a cart and walking on from the side doesn't give you as much of a chance to digest the subtle cues the green is giving you through your feet and eyes. You have to make a concerted effort to plug more of that information in before you pick your line. What comes next isn't some kind of complicated science that is hard to understand. You can go through a relatively simple process to get the feel for the line, then go with your instincts. That's where I'm trying to get you—to the point where you trust your instincts and go with them. Even if you don't pick the right line, you're going to get a better result than if you hit the putt without seeing and committing to a line.

Here's how I do it.

My first priority is to pick the basic break of the putt. On a 20-footer that goes up the side of a hill, that's an easy job. On a 10-footer that looks virtually straight, it might not be so easy. My goal is to find a break in every putt I see, so I can determine what part of the hole I want to roll the ball into.

Before I lose you, let me explain what I mean by *part* of the hole. Many people look at the line of a putt as if they were shooting a gun at the hole. The ball leaves on a line, and the line bisects the hole exactly in the hole's center. If you putt that way, you give away too much of the hole and reduce your margin for error. If the only place the ball can go into the hole is in the center, you only have the edges of the hole on either side of the center line as a place for the putt to enter.

On the other hand, if I have a 12-footer with six inches of break from right to left, I'll visualize a curve, with the ball falling into the hole at about four o'clock. On that line, if I hit it a shade too hard, the ball has a chance to drop in on the high side, at three or even two o'clock. If it's a shade too soft, it can drop in on the low side, at five or six o'clock. Not only have I given myself a much more specific target, but I've given myself a lot more space for the ball to drop in. If I aim for the center of the cup—six o'clock—and hit the putt a shade too soft, it has no chance of going in. If I hit it too hard (combined with the fact that I haven't played enough break), I'm probably going to lip it out and leave myself a downhill, sidehill comeback putt.

As I walk up and mark my ball, I'm using my eyes and my feet to determine what the predominant break is on the putt. That's an important piece of the puzzle, because I almost never play a putt longer than four or five feet dead straight. I want to see a little curve on it, and get very specific about which part of the hole I want my ball to roll into.

I've seen some players try to plumb-bob—dangle the putter from two fingers and line up the ball and the hole, looking with the dominant eye for which side the cup appears—to get a read, but even if you do it right (which is difficult), you only know which way the putt breaks, not how much. I'll try it every once in a while if I can't see a break, but you have to be really precise in how you do it or you won't get good information. If you stand behind the ball and line up the ball and hole with the shaft, when you look at the hole with just your dominant eye, it should appear on one side of the shaft or the other. The side the hole appears on is the direction the ball will break. But if you aren't standing on the extended line from the ball to the hole, or you don't keep your shoulders level while you do it, you won't get an accurate result.

Once I've determined the speed and predominant break, I move to the low side of the break—opposite the apex of the putt. In other words, if I have that same 12-footer with six inches of right-to-left break, I'll walk to the left side of the hole (from your perspective if you were watching me from behind the ball), about five steps to the side of my line, and stop at the midway point of the putt.

Why do I look at the putt from the low side? I believe it's the best position to see the complete layout of the green contours. One way to illustrate what I mean is to take a book and open it in front of you. If you tilt the book toward you, you can see everything on the page. Tilt it away from you, and you can't see much at all. It also gives you an excellent visual of the distance

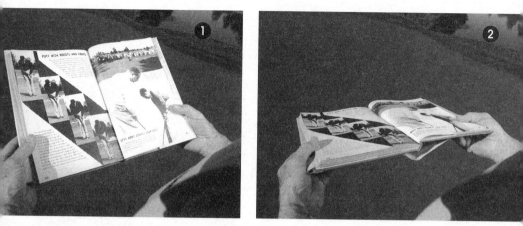

When you look at a book tilted toward you (1), you can easily see all the words and illustrations—in this case, the ones that appear in an original 1940 first edition of *Better Golf Without Practice* by Alex Morrison, the teacher who influenced my dad. When the book is tilted away from you (2), it's much harder to see any detail. When you read a putt from the low side of the break, you can see more detail than you can from the high side.

the ball needs to travel, and the pace that the ball will be rolling. You'll also be able to see subtle uphill and downhill grades more distinctly.

If I have a dramatic uphill or downhill putt, I might take a look at the putt from behind the hole as well, but usually the look from the low side is enough for me to start to pick my line.

From the low side, I break the putt into thirds, and get really interested in the last third of the putt. Whether you've got a 10-footer or a 30-footer, most of the break happens in that last third, when the ball starts to slow down. I visualize how the ball will take the curve on that last third, and exactly where it will drop into the hole.

The factors that impact speed and break are mostly what you would expect. Slope—whether it's sidehill, uphill, or downhill—and green firmness are the big ones. Firm greens cut tightly are much faster than soft greens with longer blades of grass. And the kinds of grass on the green also impact speed and break. Bermuda grass has a definite grain, and that grain runs in the direction of the setting sun—or a moderate slope, from water running down it. From just off the green, you can actually see which way the grain moves—the grass looks shiny when you're looking down-grain, and dull when you're looking into the grain. Putts will tend to move faster when they go with the grain and slower against it, and the grain will also exaggerate a break running in the same direction, or hold it up when against.

Regardless of the kind of grass, every green has a drainage area on one side, or in the front or back. On many courses, you'll actually be able to see a little plastic or metal grating. Greens are designed with a slight tilt so that rain doesn't pool on the surface. That tilt obviously impacts the overall direction putts break on the hole. It doesn't mean that every putt on that hole breaks toward the drain, but if you're stumped for a read and can't see a different break, it's good information to have. If the course is in an area with significant elevation changes, you can use that information as well. Older courses near the ocean will generally have greens that break toward the water. Greens on courses with natural rivers or lakes will tend to break toward those bodies of water, because they're the natural places for rain runoff to travel. At Augusta National, for example, putts around Amen Corner will tend to break toward Rae's Creek. Again, this information comes into play when you can't see any other obvious break. An important exception to these general rules comes on modern courses like Kiawah Island, where greens tend to break *away* from the ocean or other environmentally sensitive areas, because the designers are required to protect against chemical runoff.

How do all of these pieces of information come together to turn into a read on a given putt? It's hard for me to quantify in words specific ratios or formulas when it comes to these speed and break factors. There might be a science to hitting a tee shot with a driver, but putting is an art form. The closer you can come to making your natural, signature putting stroke, the more sensitive you're going to be to speed. Then, when you play a certain course, you'll get a feel for where the greens rate in overall speed. That feel will translate into the size of your stroke on a given putt. There's no equation for it—like taking it back a third less for a 10-footer at Augusta National than for a 10-footer at Pebble Beach. It's like the natural adjustment you make on the highway when it's wet out. You leave a little more space between you and the car ahead, to give yourself more time to react if you need to. We're going to talk some more about the characteristics of putting a true roll on the ball in Chapter Four—and how a true roll almost immediately translates into more sensitivity and speed control.

One question I get fairly often is about how specific and precise the line I visualize is. I have a two-part answer. When I make my read and visualize the line the ball takes to the hole, I'm picturing a very specific path to the hole. I'm visualizing what my ball will do. But it's important to understand that locking into a very specific visualization of your line doesn't mean you should spend ten minutes cramming every tiny bit of information about contour, grain, and green conditions into your mental computer to come up with the "perfect" read. When you hold yourself to that kind of information standard, you're going to be constantly second-guessing yourself, and that seed of doubt does much more damage to your stroke than a "perfect" read will benefit you. It's not about being perfect. If you take your first impression and go with it, you're going to be looser, and you're going to make a better stroke. In my experience, taking more time to do something that should be done in your subconscious is almost never better. And if your putt is to win something, that extra time is only going to serve to tighten you up.

A caddie can be a great help reading greens—especially when you're playing a course for the first time, but you have to decide what your relationship is going to be right from the start. If you each read the putt and don't see the same thing, you're probably going to make a stroke with some doubt in your mind. And when it comes to seeing a line, so much is dependent upon each person's perception of what the speed of the putt should be that it might be difficult to get on the same page. I think you have to commit to either reading the putt for yourself—which is what I do when I'm playing tour events—or put yourself completely in the caddie's hands when it comes to line. On tour, that's something that gets sorted out between the player and his or her caddie during practice rounds. Who is reading the greens better on a particular week? On certain occasions—usually on Bermuda—I'll go with my caddie's read, especially if he's got a lot of experience at the course.

I want to emphasize again that rolling the ball at the right speed is more important than choosing the right line. My dad taught me never to leave a putt short, but never roll it more than a foot and a half past the hole. A lot of my practice time as a kid was spent with a tee stuck in the edge of the cup at the point on the clock indicating the perfect entry spot, and another tee 18 inches behind the hole as a guide for the limit I'd want the ball to run out.

Using those two tees, you can move around the green hitting no more than two balls at a time—which we'll discuss more in depth later on—fine-tuning your ability to not only see the line, but also control your speed so that you're always around the hole. Far, far more three-putts happen because of a speed

I'll start from a crouch behind the ball to determine the main break on a putt, then move from there to the low side of the break.

mistake than a read mistake. You almost never see somebody read a putt so poorly that they miss the line by three or four feet to the left or right of the hole. The problems come when the ball dies far too short or goes rolling by hot. Developing speed control also improves your ability to visualize the ideal line, simply because you'll be getting a lot of feedback on putts that end up near the hole. You'll get tired of playing too little break— which a majority of amateur players routinely do—and missing on the low side, and you'll adjust.

After I've looked at the putt from the low side, I'll walk back behind the ball and crouch for a second or two, just to confirm what I see. I'm not rereading the putt from back there—and that's an important point. Once you're able to lock in on speed and line, don't waste that effort with the next step you take. I keep my eyes and my focus on the line during my entire pre-putt routine. My entire goal is to get set up to the ball in a way that gets me aimed to roll it on the line I'm seeing. I immediately stand up and walk in from behind the ball while making a couple of small "feel" strokes with my open right hand (and holding the putter in my left), and then I take my grip in both hands as I step in first with my right foot and then my left, all while looking at my line. I then place the putter in front of the ball (still looking at my line) and adjust my stance; my eyes come back to the ball and I lift my

My walk from my read to my stroke is designed to keep my focus on the line. I start by walking in from behind while making a small practice swing with my open right hand (1). Then I step in with my right foot, staying upright and focused on my line with both eyes (2). I set my left foot—stance slightly open, to better see the line—and keep my head up and my eyes focused on the target (3), and then I place the putter in front of the ball. I slowly tilt my head down, still looking at my line, adjust my stance, then move the putter behind the ball (4).

putter and place it behind the ball. I take one last look at the hole, my eyes focus on a spot in front of the ball, and I start my stroke. I never lose my connection to the line. And that's where a lot of players get knocked off course, literally and figuratively. Even if they go through the reading process and see the line accurately and completely, they take their focus off the line and look down at the ball while they set their feet and make a couple of practice strokes.

It happens to even the best players. When we started working with Phil Mickelson the week before the 2009 Tour Championship, his pre-putt routine consisted of taking six one-second glances at the hole, interspersed with one-second glances down at his ball, as he set his feet and before he let the putt go. I call them "glances" because that's what they are—something that's not happening for a long enough duration for you to get any information from what you're seeing. That week, he changed his pre-putt look to one long one at his target. His routine got longer—and he spent a lot of time looking at his line—but he was determined not to make his stroke until he felt comfortable. By keeping his focus on the line instead of the ball, he got to a comfort level that allowed him to make nine putts over 15 feet during the tournament, and he went on to win. Before that, in all of 2009, he had made only thirteen putts of that length or longer.

Again, it doesn't really matter to me what you do for your pre-shot routine, as long as it achieves the main goal—to allow you to translate the line you see into a roll on that line. Both Phil and Annika Sorenstam make practice strokes behind the ball, perpendicular to the line, before they get into their stances. I don't make a practice stroke—we'll talk about why in the next chapter—but if doing it at that point helps them get comfortable and stay in rhythm, I'm for it. But if making a practice stroke next to the ball either disconnects your mental picture of the line or subtly changes your aim—or both—you're not going to putt as well as you could. The most common tendency for players who take a practice stroke near the ball is that they tend to set up too square—or even closed—to the target line when they close the gap and address the ball to actually putt. That's often the difference between a make and a miss.

The last piece of advice I'll give isn't the most glamorous, but following it will produce the quickest and most positive results. Instead of spending your time practicing your stroke, devote at least 50 percent of your putting practice to seeing the line and rolling the ball on that line. In every corporate event or clinic I do, somebody pulls me aside and wants me to give them a mechanical drill they can go out and do a hundred times on the practice green and come out the other side a "better" putter.

To me, that's missing at least half the point.

Having a good stroke is useful, sure. And I want you to set up to your putt in a way that's comfortable and that helps you see the line better. But if the mental side of the game is 50 percent—and that's easily a conservative estimate—shouldn't 50 percent of your practice be on the mental and planning side?

Keep that ratio in mind as we talk about the material in this and the next two chapters. Improving your mind and your decision-making will have as much or more impact on your score than anything you do mechanically. And the ability to see the line and roll the ball on that line is something that anybody can do. There's no mystery or magic to it. Once you understand that, and believe you can do it, there's no limit to the number of putts you can make.

# THREE

# Let It Go

You're probably not reading this book because you have a shortage of information telling you what to do when it comes to putting.

And that's the basic problem.

Most players are filled up with information—some of it good, some of it bad, some of it conflicting, and most of it overwhelming—about a stroke that moves about three feet and takes up less than three seconds. The idea that you need to be thinking about so many things during the putting stroke has become so ingrained that many players don't feel comfortable unless they have that laundry list of things to think about. I'll never forget the first golf school I ever did—it was in Colorado with sixteen students over two and a half days. When we were done, one of the students sent me a letter with notes and questions, and it was more than a hundred pages long—single spaced. I couldn't believe it. He just didn't get it. He didn't realize that the process doesn't involve any kind of checklist.

You just can't play that way.

Getting from information overload to the point where you can quiet all of that and let the stroke go is the trickiest part of putting. It's more challenging than making the right read, or anything having to do with the mechanics of the stroke itself. No matter what you have going on in your head from the time you make your read until you make your stroke, the question is, how do you make sense of it, and how do you organize it in a way that actually helps you put a good roll on the ball? Accomplishing that is the secret to good putting.

In this chapter, we're going to talk about moving from seeing the line during your read to pulling the trigger on the stroke, and how to let the shot go with conviction and confidence. I'll tell you right up front that you might feel a little "naked" at first, because all of the mechanical thoughts and mostly random rituals that you go through before rolling a putt probably give you a sense of security. The pre-putt routine you use is just like any other habit—changing it is going to feel strange, at least in the beginning.

One example of this is a question I get every so often at clinics (before I've had a chance to get my hands on the players there and show them how to putt unconsciously). With a serious look on his face, a player will ask me how far back the putter should go on a 20-foot putt. That question would actually be OK if he was looking for a philosophical discussion about whether or not the putter should travel farther for a long putt, or if you should just swing harder. (The feel I like on longer putts is a longer back-swing and follow-through, not any kind of abrupt or increased accelera-tion of the putter through impact.) But what the guy usually wants is an actual measurement. He wants to know if the putter should go back to his right instep, or outside his shoe, or some other specific distance mea-surement.

Because some teachers (and golf magazines) have turned putting into this seemingly difficult-to-understand process, it's easy to see why some players would be searching for some kind of easy-to-understand guideline— a way to putt by numbers. They're looking for a way to "solve" it.

But once you start putting with more of a direct connection to feel and to your line, you're going to discover how much simpler this part of the game can be, and how much more sensitive you naturally are to speed and to the solid contact of the ball on the face of the putter. You're going to stop think-ing about exactly where your right elbow needs to be on the backswing, or how wide your stance should be, or how far back the putter needs to go, and more on the line and making your ball go there. You're going to turn putting into a more read-and-react athletic motion, versus a piece of repeating ma-chinery on an assembly line. It's certainly a simpler and more effective way to roll your ball—not to mention the fact that it's way more satisfying and fun. I don't know about you, but one of the main joys I get from this game, even to this day, is the feeling that I went out and solved the puzzle of the golf course. I used my feel and my skills to shoot a score. I didn't use some mindless, repetitive mechanical process to punch 68 shots out of the same piece of construction paper.

In the last chapter, we talked briefly about the process I go through as I walk from my read into the ball. I walk from the extended target line behind my ball, looking at the target while making a couple of small, one-handed feel strokes with my open right hand, and set my right foot first, then my left. The important point to stress here is that I'm setting my stance while at the same time visualizing the ball rolling down my target line. The two pieces are directly connected. It's important to say again, because it's a key part of being able to let it go when the time comes. When you've made a conscious decision about your line and you know you're comfortable and

I walk into my stance and set my right foot while focusing on my target line (1). I set my left foot at whatever width feels comfortable (2), and place it so that my stance is slightly open. I put my putter in front of the ball during this process as one more way to deemphasize the ball. I'm making a stroke, and the ball just gets in the way at the start of its way down my line. I look one last time at the hole, bring the putter over the ball, then I finally look down (3) in the split second before I start my stroke, but I'm not looking at the ball—I'm looking at a spot an inch or two in front of the ball. The stroke happens in my subconscious, and I'm simply watching for the ball to roll over my spot.

aimed on that line, you're one step closer to being able to let the stroke itself drop into the subconscious part of your brain.

At this point, players at every level—tour players, beginners, 10-handicappers—ask me the same question. What should the putting setup look like? My answer is always the same.

You tell me.

To be able to step up to a putt, see your line, and let it go, you need to be comfortable and confident. The pieces that go into that are different for every player, and they're even different for every player from day to day. We're going to talk about some general things to look for in setup and mechanics in the next chapter, but for the most part, I'm going to tell you to keep the setup and mechanics that feel comfortable to you. Loren Roberts, Ben Crenshaw, Phil Mickelson, and any of a half dozen other great putters all have differences in the way they set up—some subtle and some significant. Loren Roberts and Bobby Locke look like they're playing a different sport. Loren is upright and has a fairly narrow stance, and he swings the

Your stance might vary to a more narrow position (1) or a wider one (2), but I won't tell you that either one of those is wrong. I want you to have a comfortable setup position—one that makes it easiest for you to see your line.

putter straight back and straight through. Locke putted from a crouch and rolled every ball with significant hook spin.

I've been playing tournament golf for more than forty years, and my setup position, ball position, and stance width vary from tournament to tournament. Am I in the same neighborhood? Absolutely. But some days, I see the line better from a wider stance. I might even use four or five different widths in the same round—a narrower one for a fast downhill putt, and wider width for a longer one. And that's what I'm listening to—whatever setup feels comfortable and helps me see the line I've chosen.

Remember the putting signature concept from the first chapter? What you're trying to achieve here is to go from the end of your reading process—the point where you've determined your line and it's your turn to play—to the act of rolling the ball with the natural rhythm of your signature. Phil Mickelson's signature is different than mine, but we both accomplish the same things in our routine. We see the line, move into the setup, get comfortable, and let it go.

I can give you two real-world examples from the LPGA Tour. When I started working with Annika Sorenstam in 2001, she came to me with one of the best—and most recognizable—full swings in the history of the women's tour. She went at the ball very feely, letting her head go through impact to look down the line at the ball. But in putting, she had reverted to really overthinking what she wanted to do and "trying" really hard. She knew that she needed to improve her putting, and she was spending so much time thinking about mechanics and practicing that she was tied completely in knots.

We met for the first time, and she remained convinced she needed a practice swing, so we incorporated it into a routine similar to the one Phil Mickelson has adopted—where the practice swing happens back behind the ball, perpendicular to the target line, but the move into the stance is calm and deliberate and the stroke is fluid. I really wanted her to stop thinking so much when it was time to make the stroke, and by the second or third lesson it just clicked for her. And her new routine ended up matching her full swing routine just beautifully. She went on to win eight tournaments in 2001 and eight of her ten career majors in the next five years.

Taiwanese LPGA star Yani Tseng came out to see Ron and me in California late in the 2009 season after having just a miserable time in the final round of an event in Canada—forty putts. She actually stopped to see me the day after the tournament ended, on her way to the next event in Arkansas. I buckled her bag onto my cart and we drove right past the practice green and over to the first tee—which shocked her, because she had obviously thought she was going to get a putting lesson.

I asked her to take out her driver and hit a tee shot. She made a couple of loose practice swings, and then smoked it down the middle of the fairway about 265 yards without a second thought. We drove down the fairway and I dropped a ball 150 yards from the hole and asked her to hit an iron shot to the green. She knocked an 8-iron to five feet. No problem.

Once we got to the green, I pulled that ball back from five feet to about 12, and asked her to make the putt for me. You wouldn't believe how things changed. On the tee shot and the iron shot, she had gotten up there and just hit it. On the putt, her routine bogged down. She was slow and unsure, and it was absolutely no surprise that she didn't come close to making it. She was doing the same thing that Annika had done—she was "trying." She was grinding so hard over her mechanical thoughts and the desire to get better, and she was twice as critical of herself. She'd hit twice as many practice putts as she did full swing shots, and she was way, way worse at that part of the game.

I told her the simple thing we've been talking about here. You have to just let it go. See it and hit it. It's simple to say, but sometimes hard to recognize in yourself and do when you're out there in the middle of competition. I wanted her to understand which routine felt good to her—and I could see what that was in her full swing—and apply it to her putting.

The next season, she won two major championships—the Kraft Nabisco Championship and Women's British Open—and three other tournaments around the world. She's the youngest player in the history of the LPGA to win three majors, and the fastest to earn $2 million in career prize money. At twenty-two years old, she's just scratching the surface of what she can accomplish.

The ability to feel comfortable over the ball and let the stroke go isn't some secret that only experienced players can uncover. I've conducted hundreds of clinics, golf schools, and individual lessons with beginners and 20-handicappers, and it takes them about the same amount of time—thirty minutes—for those feels to click in as it does for tour players. Does that mean you can putt like a tour player in thirty minutes? Not exactly. But you can improve at the same rate. You might go from taking forty-one putts per round to thirty-five, which is the same as a tour player improving from 100th on tour to 20th.

Part of feeling comfortable and confident comes from seeing and definitively choosing your line—and preserving that visual through your pre-putt process. We talked about how your look at the line deteriorates when you continually look down at the ball. You also sabotage it when you're careless with your practice stroke. A lot of the doubt and discomfort you feel when you putt could be due to the disconnect between your read and what the ball ends up doing—and that could simply be the result of a mistake you're making during your routine.

I'll often ask a player to go through his routine, then step into the putt without taking a practice swing. I'll then put a club on the ground to show him where he's aiming. I'll then ask him to go through his regular routine, with practice swings next to the ball, and show him how making those practice putts has affected his aim (which is sometimes six or eight inches to the right, because the stance squares up too much).

Or use the example of a pool player getting ready to make a shot. Would you ever see the player stop what he or she was doing, move to the side, make a couple of practice strokes with the stick, then get back behind the cue ball and make a stroke? Absolutely not. The great pool players move the cue slowly back and forth behind the ball, visualizing the shot and *feeling* it. I like to see a player approach a putt like that pool player—staying focused on the line and staying in motion, keeping the feel in his hands. The last thing I want to see is a practice stroke routine that ends with the player stepping into the ball after he's done, placing the putter on the ground, freezing and staring down at the ball, and cycling through a series of mechanical thoughts. All of the touch and feel—and art—of the stroke are just drained away.

I just shake my head when I hear teachers or commentators say that a player needs to take his time over an important putt, or to do anything outside of the ordinary routine that the player has established from the first putt of the tournament. I've seen it happen dozens and dozens of times. A player goes through his routine with no problem on Thursday, Friday, and Saturday, but when he gets to a putt he just *has* to make, he takes more time. He fidgets over the ball, trying to get comfortable. He stares down at the ball and loses that connection with his line.

It happened to Scott Hoch and Ed Sneed in playoffs at the Masters. On the 10th hole in his playoff, Hoch got up over his putt, fidgeted a bit, then backed off. I actually yelled at the television when he did it because I knew he was going to miss. The same thing happened to Ed Sneed in 1979. He had a three-shot lead with three holes to play, and his routine completely changed. Those guys got caught up in the moment, each putt started to mean more than an "average" putt, and they started to *try*. The act of putting went from being automatic—on autopilot in the unconscious part of the mind—to conscious. To be a good putter, you need to able to treat those big ones—whether they're to make a cut, win a tour event, win a major, or win a $20 bet from your buddy—like any other putt. When I won my second PGA Championship in 1976, I had a 14-footer on the last hole to win the tournament. I went through my routine at my normal pace, and rolled my ball over that imaginary spot an inch in front. I knew it was in before it was halfway to the hole.

Another piece of that confidence comes from being much, much less obsessed about the ball. So many players change their focus from the line to the ball before making a stroke and get caught up in *hitting* it—which is like throwing a dart while focusing on your hand instead of the little circle in the middle of the dart board. They're thinking about the mechanics of the stroke, or concentrating on what the ball is going to do. I've seen it with beginners and with tour players. On every other shot, we're taught to swing the club right on through impact. The same thing is true for putting, but people get so fixated on the moment of impact that when it comes, things go haywire—and it's on a stroke that moves slow enough to where that kind of reaction can have bad consequences.

Adam Scott came to us for help last year, and when we watched him, we could see that the moment his putter hit the ball, he was lifting his hands. In a historical example, Arnold Palmer would hit the ball and recoil his putter back. Gary Player would jab at the ball with his putter and basically stop the head right at impact. They're prominent examples of what I'm talking about, but they were actually able to compete at a Hall of Fame level with those habits. It further emphasizes the point that the stroke doesn't make the player. It's all about the thought process.

The average player with the same issues tends to get so bound up in mechanical thoughts that he or she shoves the putter through impact with no sense of feel whatsoever. For those players, I simply ask them to go through their routine, and instead of looking down at the ball right before making the stroke, I ask them to keep looking at the target. It's amazing how quickly the stroke smooths out, like a snap of the fingers.

When I putt, my eyes leave the target and come down toward the ball, but I don't look at the ball. I'm looking at a spot on my line, two inches in front of the ball. I'm making an unconscious stroke, and watching my ball roll over an exact spot two inches down the target line.

In fact, you can go out to the practice green and stick a tee all the way down into the grass, two inches in front of your ball, and practice rolling the ball and actually seeing it go over the tee. Move your focus to the tee *before* you make your stroke, and watch the ball get there. After a few strokes, you won't even be thinking about the physical act of swinging the putter. Your focus is on a different place—the right place.

One last piece of letting it go that can't be overlooked has to do with attitude—a subject we're going to discuss in a lot more detail in Chapter Six. The best putters step up and let it go easily because they believe they're capable of making every putt, and they can visualize themselves performing the athletic movement. Bad putters stand over a putt with dread, run through a long list of mechanical thoughts in the hope that one or two will stick, and don't have a clear visualization of themselves making even a mediocre stroke, trying to keep something from happening.

What does that mean for you—especially if you're a 20-handicapper without much confidence in your skill level? It's a cliché, but it's true: You have to fake it before you make it. Your stroke and your results will not improve until you visualize yourself successfully making putts. Which means you need to visualize that happening before it actually happens with any regularity in your real game. Working with Yani Tseng, she'd be 10 feet from her ball and I'd tell her she needed to have the putt under way within five seconds. I'd start call it off, "one-hundred, two-hundred," and she'd literally almost run to her ball. She'd only have time for one look before she rolled

For all of the talk of about the mechanics of the putting stroke, it's an incredibly simple thing. From my address position (1), I make a forward press, swing the putter head back (2), then move the back of my left hand toward the target (3), keeping the putter head low to the ground (4). People make it out to be like trying to fly a 747 when you don't have any training. To me, it's more like steering a car. It's not something you consciously think about anymore.

the putt, but her results got so much better, because she wasn't overthinking and paralyzing her instincts.

That might sound like some kind of self-help hooey, but I'm here to tell you that it works. Throughout my entire playing career, I consistently got better results by using a series of self-talk and visualization techniques. More than once, I could directly trace a tournament win or a great round to a session that reinforced those techniques in my mind at the beginning of the week.

I make that point here because the next chapter is an overview of some basic mechanics of the putting stroke itself. I want to stress again that you can improve way more dramatically—and much faster—by working on your mind rather than working on your stroke. But some players—especially beginners—can benefit from a mechanical adjustment that makes concentrating on feel less awkward or complicated. You can putt well from a dozen different stances and with a variety of different stroke shapes. Just don't get so immersed in those possibilities that you forget the main point of all this—to put a great roll on the ball.

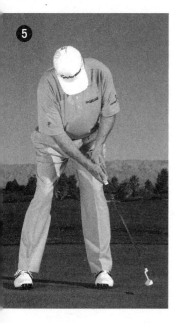

When players get overly concerned with mechanics or the ball, they tend to get really active with the putter at impact—either by hitting at it (5), or quickly looking up to see where the ball went.

# FOUR

# Roll Your Ball

The boys and I like to joke that on the list of ten things you need to putt well, the mechanics of the stroke itself are maybe seventh or eighth on the list.

But there is still a time and place to talk about stroke basics, especially for players who don't have a lot of experience—or a history of putting with any kind of feel.

And as we've been discussing in the last few chapters, feel is the major thing we're trying to achieve. My goal with any player I teach is to help them make a comfortable, effortless stroke with feel. That almost always translates into making the minimum number of mechanical adjustments necessary to improve the player's chance to feel the ball roll off the face—and absolutely no changes simply to satisfy somebody's idea of what an "ideal" setup or stroke should look like.

As far as I'm concerned, if you can see the line and roll your ball with feel on that line, your mechanics work for me.

What I'm trying to do here is describe a variety of adjustments that you can try in your setup and stroke if you *aren't* seeing the line or rolling the ball with feel. Within the parameters of the grips, stances, and strokes we're going to talk about, you should be able to find a combination that works for you—whether you're searching for a simple adjustment from week to week, or making a more substantial change.

Before we talk about those parameters, I want to make an important distinction—something that is going to help you think about your putting in a different way.

I use the word "roll" in the title of this chapter—and everywhere else in this book—very intentionally.

I hear lots of players (and commentators on television) talk about "hitting" putts, or "accelerating" the putter through impact. To me, "hitting" shouldn't be any part of putting—either in how you actually do it, or how you think about it. When I hear the word "hit," I picture the ball connecting with the face briefly, then shooting or springing off. I think of a hockey player hitting a slap shot, or a baseball player crushing a home run. I see it when I watch a bad putter stand over a three-footer and try to jam it in the back of the hole to "take the break out of it."

None of that equates to feel.

I want you to get into the mind-set of *rolling* your ball, not hitting it. I want you to go into each putt trying to keep the ball on the face for as long as possible, so you can feel it. Putting is a finesse move. I'm trying to get you to *feel*. To be the .350 hitter who finds the hole between first and second base, not the home run hitter. To feel yourself rolling the ball and dropping it in the cup—so that if you do happen to miss, you're not going to have very much to do to finish up. Picture Ben Crenshaw or Bob Charles, and how soft their hands are as they roll it. That's rolling it with feel.

And accelerating? It's true that you don't want to *de*celerate, but all of my thoughts are about making a smooth, rhythmic stroke. I'm not thinking about how fast or how slow it's going. To equate it to driving a car, I'm not jamming the accelerator down trying to record a fast 0-to-60 time. I'm driving a consistent 30 miles per hour, listening to calm music.

So when we talk about some of the physical parameters of the stroke here, keep in mind the overall goal—feel and rhythm, not effort and acceleration.

I don't believe in a cookie-cutter setup position or actual putting stroke, but I have a definite idea of what I like to see in a player's grip. There's some room for variation—as long as the basic idea of balance is still there.

What does balance in a grip mean? In a perfectly balanced, neutral grip, both thumbs run down the top of the handle, the back of the left hand is aimed directly at the target and the back of the right hand is parallel to the back of the left—and aimed straight away from the target.

When the hands turn on the handle away from neutral, there's the potential to lose "balance." If you keep that left hand in the neutral position, but turn the right hand on the handle so that the back of the hand is pointed more at your right shoe, you've made your right-hand grip stronger. If you keep your right hand in the neutral position, but turn your left hand on the handle so that the back of it points more toward your left foot, you've made your left-hand grip weaker.

You can move the left hand into that weaker position, so the thumb runs on the target side of the handle, as long as the right hand moves into a stronger position on the other side of the hand, so that the right thumb is on the opposite side. There's still balance there.

You start to think about your stroke a lot more than I like when you lose the balance in your grip. When one hand is turned away from neutral and the other doesn't balance it out, you change the relationship between the hands and how they work together in a putting stroke. Think about it: If you only had one arm, you'd learn a smooth, flowing swing out of necessity. You'd have no other way to get the putter to move through impact. It's only when the second arm gets involved that you're faced with having the two hands and arms work together.

For example, some of the tour players I see have the left hand on the club in a nice neutral position and the right hand turned into a slightly too strong position, away from the target. They look down and see the hands as "neutral." But when the right hand is too strong, that grip presets the right hand in a position to get really active through the stroke, like it would be in a full swing. And adding that kind of "hit" is not conducive to good speed control. You want the right hand to have feel and to control distance, but you don't want it to take over the whole stroke.

Once you've established balance in your grip, you link your hands together on the grip. The three most common ways to do that (not counting alternative grips like cross-handed or the claw, which we'll talk about a little later in this chapter) are to use the same grip you would on a full shot (overlapping or interlocking), a reverse overlap grip, or a 10-finger grip.

Personally, I use (and like to see) a reverse overlap grip—where the left index finger rests on top of the right hand, in between the knuckles of the pinky and ring fingers. I think that grip maintains the balanced relationship between the left and right hands and makes it easy for the back of the left hand to lead and move straight toward the target.

When I place my hands on the grip, I spread my fingers slightly, to cover as much of the handle as I can—but I don't extend the index finger of my right hand. The club is in all of the fingers of my right hand, to be more sensitive to feel and speed, and more along the lifeline of my left hand, which is my guide hand. I can feel all of my fingers on the handle, with the firmest contact points coming between my index finger and thumb on my right hand, and the last three fingers of my left hand.

When I say "contact points," I'm talking about using only enough grip pressure to keep the handle of the putter from falling out of my hands. How much pressure? I can't give you a number on a dial or anything like that, but something Sam Snead said about the full-swing grip really holds true for putting. He said he wanted his grip to feel like he was holding a baby bird in his hand tight enough to prevent the bird from escaping, but not so tight that he crushed it. So many players would absolutely crush the bird—because they're tense and nervous, their hands don't cover enough of the grip, or they've been taught to try to freeze the hands and rock the shoulders to hit a putt. To me, that absolutely robs you of your ability to feel and judge distance. If you touched my hands when I was set up to putt, you'd immediately feel that they were loose and soft—so much so that it would almost feel as if you could pull my hands off the club. I want my hands soft and the club to feel very light (and actually *be* light, which we'll talk more about in Chapter Seven).

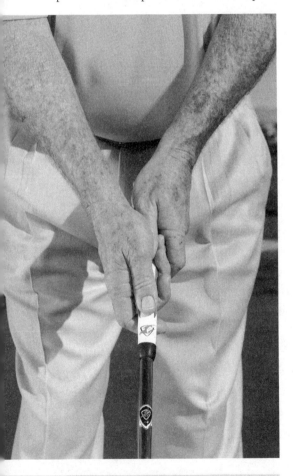

My hands are soft, tension free, and spread over most of the grip. I use the reverse overlapping putting grip—with the index finger of my left hand resting between the pinky and ring fingers of my right hand, and the shaft is parallel to the zipper on my pants.

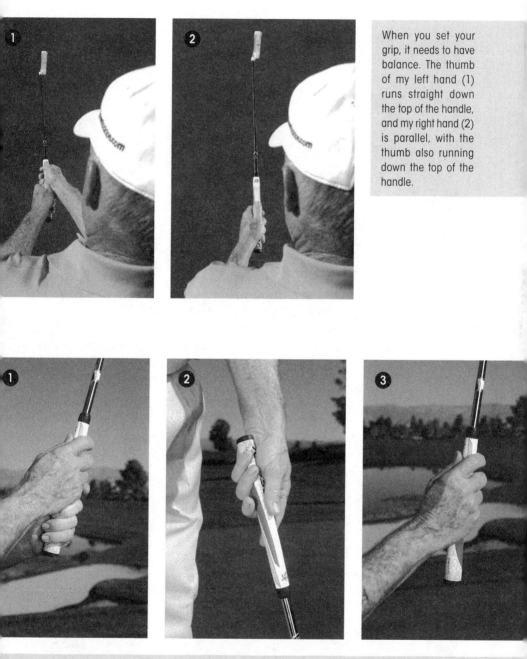

When you set your grip, it needs to have balance. The thumb of my left hand (1) runs straight down the top of the handle, and my right hand (2) is parallel, with the thumb also running down the top of the handle.

These photographs show the looseness of my grip. You can't see any tension in my left hand (1), and there's some space between my fingers. Notice the contact of my fingertips on the handle (2). This is where feel comes from. In the right hand, the grip runs more down the lifeline, rather than in the fingers (3).

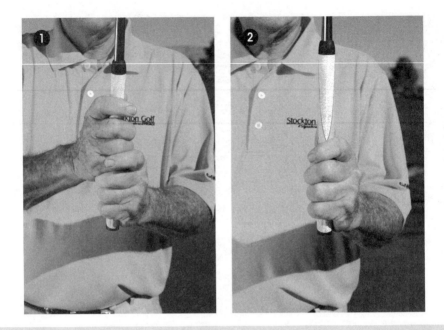

Some players link their hands in their standard full-swing grip, or overlap two fingers of the left hand on top of the right hand. I like to have my left index finger as the only overlapping part of my grip (1). The side of my left palm rests at the end of the handle (2), not the little finger on my left hand. The fingers on my right hand cover almost all of the rest of the grip (3). When I put the putter down (4), my left wrist is flat and straight.

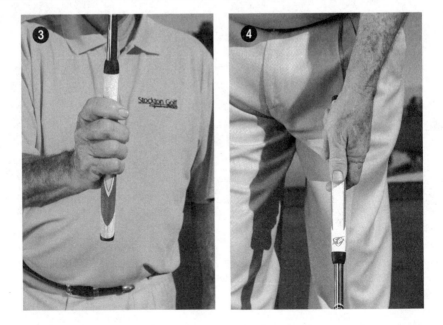

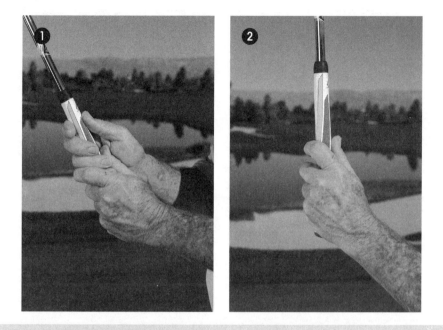

Here you can see the way my left and right hands link together on the club (1). The tension points on the handle are the last three fingers of my left hand (2) and between the spot on the handle where the thumb and forefinger of my right hand come together (3). If I hold the putter in just the last three fingers of my left hand (4), I should be able to make smooth, one-handed strokes.

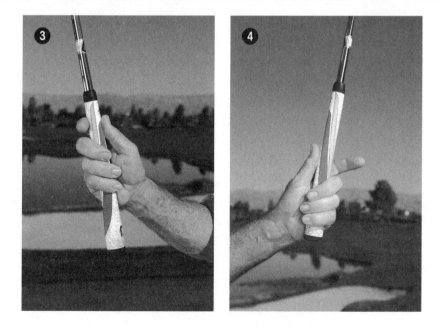

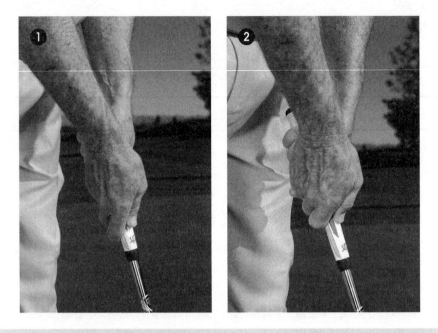

I like the hands to cover the grip, and for the shaft to be an extension of the left arm (1). When the hands squeeze together on the grip (2), it introduces tension—a feel killer. Notice how the handle has dropped below my forearms, creating an angle between the shaft and my arms.

To get a more appropriate sensation for a good putting grip, get in your putting stance and hold a ball between the thumb and index finger on your right hand. Now smoothly toss the ball underhanded toward a target 15 feet away, using just your arm and wrist. Notice how your fingers stayed soft, and there was no tension or jerky movements. You instinctively held the ball in your fingertips, and used some slight wrist action to send the ball on its way. Another way to think about it is the way you'd throw a dart—using the same combination of index finger and thumb to secure the dart loosely and deliver it with touch and feel at the board. Putting is no different—except when players override their natural instincts and get rigid and mechanical.

With a neutral, loose, tension-free grip, you can get to the top of the back-swing and simply let the putter go. You don't have to pull with the hands or throw the head at the ball. There's no manipulation—just gravity.

If you decide to use your same full-swing grip (or the 10-finger grip, for that matter), that's fine if you get more feel that way—but you need to guard against a few common problems associated with those grips. If you interlock the index finger on your left hand with the pinky finger of your right, or if you overlap your right pinky on top of the left hand, you'll tend to create more tension in the hands. As I said, tension is a feel killer. You also need to be careful that whatever grip style you use doesn't push the handle of the putter into the meaty part of your palms. You're destroying whatever sense of feel you might have that way.

A putting grip can often evolve as a series of compensations for *perceived* problems in the stroke—and the "cure" ends up causing more problems than the original "problem." Take the player who understands that the fingertips are where feel is. He decides to extend the index finger on his right hand down the shaft to get more feel. I'm all for increasing feel, but when you extend the finger that way, you virtually guarantee that the right hand will dominate the stroke. The right hand will fire during the stroke, making it really hard to have any kind of consistent distance control. At the other end of the spectrum, the player who understands that leading with the left hand will improve his distance control decides to overlap both the index and middle finger of his left hand on top of his right—or extends the index finger of the left hand to run across all four fingers on the right. Each of those methods, unfortunately, shrinks both the amount of coverage the hands have on the handle and the number of fingers doing the controlling. That almost always results in increased tension—and less feel.

My dad taught me how to hold the putter sixty years ago, and I've never made any modifications to the grip he taught me. That might lead you to believe that I'm old-fashioned, or that I look down on some of the alternative grips that players use. It's actually the opposite. I'm in favor of any kind of grip that increases your particular comfort level and sense feel. I've seen players use the cross-handed grip and the claw, and each of these grips can produce great results.

Players who struggle to keep the right hand from dominating the stroke (or from messing it up with a twitch, in a case of the yips) often switch to a cross-handed grip. In the most common cross-handed style, the player simply reverses hand positions on the handle so that the right hand is above the left, and the last two fingers of the left hand rest in the space between the thumb and index fingers of the right hand.

The claw grip operates on the same overall principle—getting the right hand to quiet down during the stroke. In this grip, the left hand sits on the handle in the conventional way, but the right hand turns so that the side of the palm and the top of the thumb rest along the handle, while the hand itself stays open and the palm faces your knees. Holding the club like this, the right hand can't do anything except act as an extension of the right arm and push the club toward the target. Since the fingers on the right hand aren't wrapped around the handle, the right hand can't turn or twist the handle and mess up the stroke.

I like the cross-handed grip better than the claw, because you still have feel in the fingers of both hands that are on the handle. But if it takes some modified version of the claw to help you feel comfortable with the putter in your hands, I'm all for it. For example, Dean Wilson doesn't use the claw, but he has an extreme grip, with both hands turned dramatically under the club and his elbows sticking out. He had come to see me for chipping, but I just had to know how he got to the putting stance he was using. He described how well it helped him see the line, and he demonstrated it by rolling his ball unbelievably well. That was all I needed to hear, and I didn't say another word to him about it. I don't teach a method. I want players to get better using what they have.

In the cross-handed grip (1), the right hand moves to the top of the grip, while the left hand replaces it below. Moving the left hand low (2) makes it the lead hand in the stroke, and restricts the right wrist from breaking down. Notice how the thumbs still run down the top of the handle, as in a standard grip.

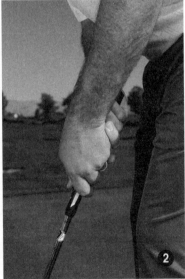

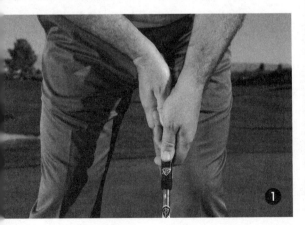

Another way to restrict the right hand from firing or otherwise moving too much through the stroke is to change the angle of the wrist (1). With the claw, the right hand faces palm down, instead of palm-to-target, and the side of the right index finger and hand contact the handle. With the right hand turned this way (2), the wrist can't bend—however, you also lose the feel associated with holding the handle in the fingers.

Bernhard Langer is winning events right now on the Champions Tour with a long putter, and he had a long and successful career before that using a variety of putting grips—including one where he bent over and held the handle of the putter against his left forearm. It's all about finding the place where feel and comfort meet.

That same idea—feel and comfort—is also the key when it comes to your stance and posture. As we discussed in the last chapter, I believe that it's easier to see the line with a slightly open stance. How open? My left foot ends up being an inch or two farther away from the target line than my right foot. It's more about the feel of being slightly more turned toward the target than it is a specific distance. But if you open your stance too much, you start to create a situation in which your arms and hands can't make an unconscious stroke. They have to shove the putter out and away from your body to push the ball on line. As we talked about before, a perfectly square stance makes it harder to see the line accurately, and a closed stance blocks your arms from moving freely in front of you. When that happens, you have to flip the putterhead at the ball—a distance-control killer.

When I get into my stance, I don't think about a specific distance that my feet should be apart, or the amount of crouch I need to get into. I want my arms to feel loose in front of me, so I bend over at the hips and flex my knees enough to get that feel. You don't want a bunch of body movement in a putting stroke, but at the same time, you don't want to be tense and rigid as you struggle to shut down any movement except the arms. In reality, the putting stroke is a pretty small movement that doesn't require much muscle power. I would call my posture and stance stable, athletic, and comfortable. I'm not crouched, like Arnold Palmer, or upright like Loren Roberts.

My ball position does stay relatively consistent, both front to back (toward the target or away from it) and, in the distance from my body, out to in. If I held a ball in front of my right eye—my dominant eye—and dropped it, it would land on the ball I was about to putt. Most players would drop the ball and have it land to the inside of the ball they were going to putt, which means they're looking at the line from a distorted view. By both opening your stance slightly and setting up with your weight on the balls of your feet and a little more tilt to your hips, you'll shift your upper body so that your head is over the ball, keeping your eyes over or slightly behind the ball. I would rather the ball position be too far back in the stance than too far forward. The ball can stay on the face of the putter for a longer period of time. Too far forward and you'll tend to pop your putts, or worse yet recoil on them. And if you're going to make a mistake in terms of the ball being too close or too far away, err on the side of too close, because the farther away it gets, the more the stroke turns into an arc like the full swing.

How important is it to know which eye is dominant? Ask anybody who shoots a gun for sport. If you set up so that you're looking down the sight of the gun with your nondominant eye, you'll struggle to hit a single bird. But if you shift and look down the sight with your dominant eye, your ability to judge the path of the moving target significantly improves. To figure out which eye is dominant, stretch your arms out in front of you and make a diamond with your index fingers and thumbs. Using both eyes, center the diamond over an object in the distance. Now, first close your right eye and then your left. When you close your dominant eye, the object in the center of the diamond will move. Close your nondominant eye and you'll still see the object in the center of the diamond.

Even though my ball position stays consistent, my stance might get slightly

How close (1) or far (2) from the ball you stand impacts your ability to swing on a consistent path—and to see the line accurately. With the ball close, the putter will tend to move on a more restricted, straight path. I like to play the ball underneath my dominant eye—which gives me room to make my natural stroke and to see the line with the least distortion. To find the right distance, set up in your stance and hold a ball just in front of your dominant eye (3). When you drop it (4), it should land on the ball on the ground.

wider or narrower depending on how I feel on a certain day or over a certain putt. As I said before, we're not machines. Putting well is about absorbing information and making good decisions based on the way your hands and body feel on a given hole or a given day—not by being some kind of robot.

With the ball in a consistent, centered position under your eye line, the putter should naturally set up in an ideal position—with the shaft in a position in which the handle is neither shifted toward the target nor angled away from it, and the sole is flat on the ground. (If the sole isn't flat on the ground, you probably need to bend the putter to adjust it, which we'll talk about in Chapter Seven). Many players who lean the putter back, away from the target, do it because their putter doesn't have enough loft on it. When I see somebody with that setup, I usually just hand them my putter; they see the loft and instinctively make a forward press, because they subconsciously feel as if they don't have to do anything to get the ball rolling.

I like a neutral start position, where you can make a rhythmic forward press. When you start with the handle forward at address (1), you're taking all the loft off the putter when you make the forward press, and you'll have trouble putting a good roll on the ball. Players often set the handle back, away from the target (2), as a reaction to using a putter with too little loft. Switching to a putter with 4 or 5 degrees of loft often fixes this address problem automatically.

Putting success is determined by how well you sort out the speed and break of your putt and translate the read into the roll of the ball. It's about using your head and then getting out of your own way emotionally.

When you sign your name to a scorecard, you do it without a conscious thought about how you move your hand and fingers. But if I asked you to go back and copy your signature exactly, your signature would go from an unconscious move to a conscious one. I want you to putt like you write your original signature, not the copy.

Your stance and set-up should suit you and your body, but some grip basics are universal. The hands should be balanced on the handle (1), meaning the back of the left hand is aimed straight at the target, and the back of the right is aimed straight away. I link my hands together using the reverse overlap grip (2), where the left index finger rests on top of the fingers of my right hand, between the knuckles of the pinky and ring fingers. When I set my grip, I spread my fingers slightly (3) to cover more of the handle—for feel—but I do not extend my right index finger down the shaft. This promotes a hitting action, not a roll.

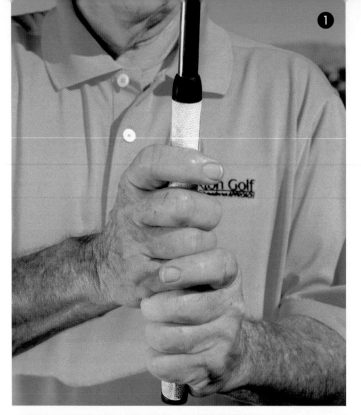

A consistent routine is a key element to unconscious putting. The first part is the read. I start from behind the ball (1) to determine the overall break. Once I do that, I walk to the low side of the break to begin visualizing my line. As I step into my stance (2), I don't take my eyes off my line, and I make small practice swings with my right hand for feel. I step in with my right foot first, then left, all while staying upright and looking at my line, and I place my putter in front of the ball (3). I move the putter back behind the ball, look down at a spot just in front of my ball, and let it go. I never lose connection to my line.

There have been great putters who used a wide variety of strokes—from straight-back straight-through to arc, from an open stance to a closed one, and from a super upright posture to a crouched one. How you stroke it mechanically is not as important to me as feeling comfortable over the ball and having a consistent routine. I make a forward press (1) at the start to give the stroke a dynamic beginning, swing the putter back (2), and concentrate on moving the back of my left hand toward the target (3) and keeping the putterhead low to the ground (4).

If you want to get the most out of your putting practice time, my advice for you isn't going to be the most exciting. Instead of obsessing about your mechanics or standing over a hundred five footers, spend at least 50 percent of your time going through your full routine: picking your line, and rolling the ball directly over a tee just in front of your ball and watching your putt roll over the line you chose. You're building the connection between seeing the line and rolling the ball on that line—which is a mixture of direction and speed control.

One of the keys to better distance control is rolling the ball instead of hitting it. Hold your left shoulder with your right hand and make some one-handed strokes (1) to keep the left shoulder level, the putterhead low, and the left hand in control. By keeping the shoulder low and the putterhead close to the ground, you avoid the hit move (2) that comes when you flip your hand at the ball.

You need to be very specific in how you visualize your line—including picking the spot where the ball will drop into the cup. One way to practice this skill is to set up a 10- or 12-foot putt with about six inches of break, and stick a tee in the cup where you believe the ball should drop in the cup. Instead of simply trying to make the putt, try to bounce the ball off the tee.

You should feel like the handle is directly in front of and parallel to the zipper on your pants, with the putter itself working as almost an extension of your left arm. Many players set the hands low at address—often because the ball is too far away—which creates an angle between the club and the arms and encourages the right hand to be very active in the stroke. That's usually a recipe for misses to the left.

The last piece of advice I have for the pre-stroke part of the puzzle relates to the feel of what the shoulders should do. My goal is to make a stroke moving my left hand toward the target, with the putter staying low to the ground through the finish. If you start with your shoulders tilted so that the left is much higher than the right, you're going to be far more likely to flip the hands or pull the putter up through impact—or to lift out of your posture too early. I like to feel as if my left shoulder is low, or "heavy," at address. In fact, to help players get that feel in the left shoulder, I'll sometimes stand across from them while they hit practice putts and hold their shoulder down to keep it from rocking during the stroke. I also have a great drill that my dad taught me that will help you practice that exact feel, and I'll show it to you at the end of the book.

I really hesitate to talk too much about the stroke itself, because I don't want you to get distracted from the main goal that we've been talking about over and over again here. If you can see the line and get the ball rolling on that line, the *quality* of the roll you put on the ball doesn't matter as much. I have always rolled the ball well, but I know I would be a good putter even if I had a "bad" roll. I might not be quite as consistent, because the ball wouldn't be coming off the middle of the face every time, but my overall results would be just fine. My son Ronnie always says that people get distracted by the quality of my roll, and think that copying my stroke is the quickest way to get better. In reality, changing how and what you *see* and *feel* is the trick. The quality of my routine is my secret weapon.

That fact is why I want to emphasize here the parts of the stroke that promote feel and rhythm, and spend less time talking about things like path and length of backstroke. You don't trace a putting stroke. You feel it, and that's what I'm trying to give to you.

The physical challenge in putting is to go from a quiet, static, information-gathering position to a fluid motion while keeping the visual of your line in your head. You need to have a trigger that bridges the gap. That's where the forward press comes in.

A forward press is the slight, smooth shifting of the handle of the club toward the target—while the clubhead end of the putter stays in place. I really like a forward press for a variety of reasons. First, it gives the stroke a dynamic starting point, instead of a cold start from a frozen position. It also provides a rehearsal of the move I'm going to make during the stroke itself—moving the left hand into the hole (so to speak), right down the target line.

I'm describing the forward press as something that happens before the stroke itself, but in real time, it's actually a piece of the backswing. I make a slight shift of the handle a couple of inches toward the hole, and as soon as that motion starts, my left index finger triggers the movement of the putterhead into the backswing.

There are no hard and fast rules about the amount or the speed of your forward press. It should work as a matching piece of your full stroke—and the stroke should be a continuation of it. If you have a short, fast stroke, your forward press is probably going to be shorter and faster than one used by a player who has a longer, slower stroke. The only caution I'd give you about this move is to watch that you don't press the handle off your target line. If you shift the handle to the right of the target line, you'll turn the face to the right (and vice versa if you shift to the left).

If you need more proof of how important a forward press is to the putting stroke, look at Phil Mickelson. Phil was a fantastic putter all through his junior and college career, and he did it with a pronounced forward press. He gradually reduced it during his professional career as he added layers of mechanical thoughts to his routine, and by the time I saw him in 2009, he was pretty far away from the natural, intuitive genius he had shown with the putter.

We already talked about how Phil simplified his pre-putt routine and changed the series of brief looks at the hole with more extended focus on his line. The second piece of the puzzle for him was returning to a more flowing, natural start to his putting stroke. Getting back to the forward press helped him reconnect with the feel that was always there. His stroke went back to a more reactive, athletic motion. He started putting more unconsciously.

So many books and instruction stories have been written about the putting stroke itself, and I believe they all mean well. But the problem with al-

When I make a stroke (1), I'm not thinking about tracing any path, or about anything mechanical at all. I'm thinking about solid contact and moving the back of my left hand low and toward the target. Notice how low the putter stays to the ground after impact (2).

most all of them is that they're attempting to get players to trace an "ideal" stroke instead of helping them develop a sense of feel and touch with the stroke they have.

I'm not going to tell you that you should swing the putter in an arc or take it straight back and straight through. To be honest, I don't think swing path matters very much as long as the putter is moving straight down the target line at impact and the face is square at impact. That might be frustrating for some players to hear. I've done plenty of clinics with players who want to know exactly how far to take the putter back and on what line to swing it—exactly what line.

The reality is, I used to take the putter back a little outside and loop it around, and now I take it back a little to the inside. Ben Crenshaw brings it back on an arc to the inside. Loren Roberts brings it back straight. We've all made a ton of putts over a lot of years, doing it with different mechanics. And from talking to a lot of world-class putters over the years, I can tell you that even the best can't run through a laundry list of mechanical thoughts, trace a swing path, *and* focus on where they want the ball to go. It's just too much to do in too short a time.

I'm not suggesting that your stroke is completely unimportant. I'm just saying that if you made a list of the ten most important factors in making putts, mechanics would ninth or tenth. You can spend as much time as you want on the practice green, but I can tell you that I haven't spent more than twenty minutes at a time there, aside from when I'm teaching, in the past thirty years.

See the line, make your forward press, and swing the back of the left hand down the target line. Give your feel a chance to emerge.

# FIVE

# Why You Three-Putt

Golf is a challenging game, and there are certainly plenty of ways to give away shots. But there's a different kind of pain and aggravation attached to three-putting. The hole is so close, and it feels like such a *waste*.

We've all done it. At the 1970 PGA Championship at Southern Hills, I was paired with Arnold Palmer in the last round. I three-putted the fifth hole for bogey, and somebody yelled from the gallery, "You've got him now, Arnie." The goal is to understand what factors go into three-putting, and to do whatever you can to reduce the likelihood—and forget about it immediately after it happens. After the three-putt at Southern Hills, I made two birdies and an eagle (and a double-bogey) over the next four holes to expand my lead from four to seven, and I went on to win the tournament.

We've talked a lot about signature and routine when it comes to standing over a particular putt. Here, I want to talk about some of the big-picture issues when it comes to putting. Just like on the rest of the hole from tee to green, the strategy you use helps determine how successfully you get from point A to point B.

I'll give you an example. You're playing a 520-yard par-5 with a double dogleg. There's water down the left side of the hole off the tee, but you can try to cut off some of it with an aggressive line and have a chance to reach the green in two. The score you make is in large part determined by the strategy you take, especially in terms of how that strategy relates to your skill level. If you're a short hitter, or you're wild off the tee, the higher percentage play would be to hit a shorter club in the fairway, hit a second shot in the layup area, and try to get up and down for your birdie.

Tour players are obviously extremely talented, but one factor that separates them from the average player just as much as their talent level does is an understanding of how important it is to avoid trouble in the first place, and to get out of it as soon as possible when you're in it. Tour players hit a bad shot and make a par or a bogey. They don't usually get out of position on the hole, try for the miracle recovery, and make double- or triple-bogey.

That's a philosophy that can help you in every part of your game, but especially on the green. A major, major step in your development as a putter is to be able to accurately assess the situation you're in and pick the line based on the proper speed that will either put you in the hole or leave you with a simple tap-in.

I realize that's easier said than done, but let me explain.

We'll start with the basic distinction between line and speed. When an amateur player goes into his read and his routine, he's almost always focusing most of his energy on the line. He either wants to be "aggressive"—in which case he plays a straighter line and tries to jam it in the back of the hole—or he doesn't really know what he's looking for in the read, so he guesses and puts a tentative stroke on it. With either of these situations, the most likely outcome is a putt that runs five feet past the hole or one that stops five feet short.

Let's remember what the game really is. You can see the hole over there, and you're trying to make the ball go into the hole, or leave it as close to it as possible. I'm always thinking about making the putt or, if I don't, leaving it no more than 18 inches past. Am I focusing on my line? Absolutely. But I'm focusing on speed even more. The fact is, speed is even more important when it comes to avoiding three-putts. Comparatively few three-putts happen because of a bad read on the line. It's bad speed.

Some players hear me talk about rolling the ball with the idea that it will fall into the cup—or end up just past the hole—and think I'm a "passive" or "lag" putter. I don't see it as being defensive at all. I'm just more specific about how far I want the ball to go, and I understand the consequences of making more of a hit in an effort to jam the ball in. For every putt you make because you took the break out of it, you'll leave yourself a couple of comeback putts from too far that probably you'll miss.

When we run our putting clinics at clubs and resorts around the country, we'll sometimes start by asking the group about the relative importance of speed versus line. Amateur players will even answer the right way most of the time—that speed is the most important. But when you ask those same players how much of their routine is devoted to determining pace, they almost always don't have an answer.

Speed or pace seems to be a mystery, yet it's the piece of the puzzle that's right out there in front of you. To read break and see your line, you have to make a series of judgment calls. The location of the hole out there in front of you is 100 percent tangible. You can see how far the ball has to go to get to the hole. It should be the easier part of the putt to judge, yet people don't think of it that way.

Does that mean I want you to go and step off all of your putts to have an exact idea of distance, and calibrate that distance to an exact size of your stroke? Absolutely not. I'm trying to liberate your feel, not make you a slave to some set of calculations. If you dedicate more of your routine to focusing on distance, you're going to discover that your brain is very capable of judging distance almost subconsciously.

We've already talked about how to read putts, but another crucial piece of green reading is seeing the entire green and where the difficult putts on that green are. As I mentioned earlier, when I was growing up, people putted better because they walked and carried their own bag or used a caddie. Why is that important? An experienced caddie could certainly help with a read or two, but the answer is even simpler than that. When players walked, they came up onto every green on foot and could get a sense for what the green did as a whole. How firm was the grass? Where was the drainage area for water to run off? Where were the prevailing slopes and humps? None of these things are conscious calculations. They're just things that go into the mental computer subconsciously and help inform the read—and the decision about how to play the putt.

But when most players get to the green and see that they have a 40-footer, they either walk up and give it a whack with no thought at all about what they should be trying to do, or they walk around it seven different ways, get paralyzed by all of the information, and make a tentative stroke.

Think about it. That first putt counts on your scorecard the same as a 250-yard tee shot, or the great hybrid club you hit onto the green. You probably don't walk up onto the tee and swing away with your driver without any thought about where you're trying to go, or what the potential trouble spots are in front of you. And you don't walk up to an approach shot, grab a random club out of the bag without looking at the number on the bottom, and disregard all of the design features surrounding the green. If there's a pond to the left of the fairway or a creek running in front of the green, those factors absolutely play a part in your decision-making. Just because the trouble spots are less obvious on the green surface itself doesn't mean you shouldn't be paying attention to them.

Let's start with the simplest distinction. If you have that 40-footer we were just talking about, and it's uphill, would it be better to hit the putt too hard and end up five feet past the hole, or be slightly short (even though my goal is to never leave it short)? It's far better to be slightly short, leaving yourself with an easy, uphill tap-in. If you knock the ball five feet by, you all of a sudden have a tricky five-foot downhill putt coming back, which means you're leaving yourself far more work than if your mistake is an inch or two short of the hole. So maybe your goal on that 40-footer is to leave it no more than 8 to 12 inches past the hole, instead of 18. The reverse is true on a downhill putt. If you get nervous about the speed and make your mistake short of the hole, you're left with another downhill putt. A mistake a little long is the better one to make.

An interesting side note to the whole uphill-downhill conversation is the idea of personal preference. On a four- or five-footer, most players would say that they prefer an uphill putt, because they can be more "aggressive" with it. I actually prefer downhill putts, because I know they're going to get to the hole and I can concentrate on my stroke and just roll it. If I'm a little strong, then I have a little uphill putt coming back. But if I have an uphill putt, I have to use more stroke on it and roll it a little more firmly. There's a chance I could go past and have a trickier putt coming back. How you feel about each of those putts has to fit in with your strategy for playing on every green. You're picturing making every putt, but you're also picturing leaving yourself with putts that you can deal with if you don't make the first one.

As you get closer to the hole, three-putts stop happening because of pace and start happening because of confidence level and expectation. Confidence is a great—and important—thing, and everything we've been talking about in this book is geared toward getting you to feel more confident about your putting. Feeling confident about your stroke and your process is calming, and it helps you perform at a higher level.

Expectation is a different beast.

If you surveyed a hundred average players about whether they feel more comfortable over an eight-footer or a 15-footer (and attached them to a magic truth-telling machine), I bet the vast majority would say they feel more comfortable over the 15-footer.

Why? Expectation.

On a 15-footer, you can walk up to the ball, get engrossed in your routine and your process, and make your roll. You hope it goes in, but you're not "supposed" to make all of your 15-footers. If you make it, you're happy. If you have a tap-in two-putt, that's OK, too. It's "par."

But when you get closer to the hole—to the point where you can see it out of the corner of your eye as you stand over your putt and look down at the ball—all of a sudden, you start to sweat a bit. You're feeling like you're within the range where you should make it, and you're thinking about the negative consequences if you miss. The consequence could be missing out on birdie when you hit it in tight, or saving par when you chipped it up. It could be losing a bet, or missing out on a scoring milestone you were trying for. It could just be feeling like you're no good, or that you failed.

That's the start of the negative self-talk cycle that traps so many players—and for some, it can even be the genesis of the yips, which are a physical manifestation of trying too hard or caring too much.

I've never had the yips, but I'm familiar with that negative self-talk cycle. When I first turned pro, I only hit seven or eight greens per round. My short game was excellent, so I hit a lot of chip shots close to the hole. As a result, I made a lot of putts, because I had a lot of short putts to make. I improved my long game after a couple of years, and started hitting ten or eleven greens. On those greens, I had longer putts, so my total number of putts went up and my scores stayed pretty much the same—which was frustrating.

One way we test players for this sense of expectation is to ask them to start out with a putt to nothing—just stroking it out to the middle of the practice green, with no specific target. As they roll those putts, we ask them what they're thinking about, and how quiet their mind is. They'll almost always say they're thinking about nothing. They're just blank. Then we'll take a ball and put it five feet from the hole, and tell them that they've just hit an approach shot in there and have the putt for birdie. Is the mind still blank? At that point, most players admit that they're not as quiet in the mind at that point.

Tour players can be even more of a challenge because they have a high capability level and a lot of talent, and they also usually believe that they're much quieter and more solid with their routine than they really are. At that point, you have to try to show them that that isn't the case.

To try to eliminate some of that sense of expectation, we'll have players simply set up over the putt, see the line, and roll the ball over their spot an inch in front of the ball, without worrying about any target. And we'll do this over and over again, just like learning how to start a car and put it in gear. We're not worried about driving or steering, just getting started. They start to realize that the better they get at focusing on that part—rolling it over the spot—and not the consequences, the more their putts go in. They achieve success as a by-product of this process, not as a direct result of "trying" to make the putt.

As the target gets closer, many players feel this almost irresistible impulse to try to control the stroke and make it precise and perfect. There's no such thing as perfect, and you don't have to be perfect for the ball to go in. The stress and anxiety of *trying* so hard to be perfect actually gets in the way of being good.

For those players, I'll set them on a straight putt of about eight feet, stick a tee in the middle of the front edge of the cup and tell them to hook a putt in around the right side of the tee, then cut one in around the left side. At first, they'll look at me funny and wonder if I've lost my marbles. But once their competitive streak is exposed and they start playing the game, they rediscover all the feel in their hands. They realize that the game is rolling the ball with touch, not tracing a blueprint with a mechanical pencil. It's about signing your name, not copying it. And better yet, once you pull that tee out of the cup, the hole looks huge. It feels like you've got all the room in the world to roll a ball in.

I was out at an LPGA event recently, and what I saw from two particular players—both extremely successful—fits exactly with what we're talking about here. One player I had never worked with, and the other I've known—and helped—for years.

The player I had never worked with was on the practice green with a little collection of balls and one of those wooden stroke guides on the grass in front of her. She was hitting one four-footer after another, uphill, and just banging them into the cup. I wanted to walk over and kick that stroke guide out of the way and ask her to just calm down and try to die a few putts into the hole. Nothing she was doing remotely resembled touch or feel.

You don't need a crystal ball to see what comes out of that kind of practice. When you get out on the course and have a four-footer like that, you hit it firm and expect it to slam into the cup, but it does a power lip out and goes four feet past the other way. You're so shocked and embarrassed that you probably end up missing that one, too. And worse, it makes you start to second-guess yourself, and you lose confidence. You lose your positive self-talk, and your attitude is reflected in your results. It's frighteningly easy to get caught up in that cycle.

The other player has been a friend for years—Juli Inkster—and I watched her make a really uncharacteristically bad stroke the week before, on the last hole. The putterhead must have been eight inches off the ground at the finish on a putt that might have been five feet long, and she missed it. I saw her the next week, and I caught her eye later and asked her jokingly if she had forgotten my number. We talked about how hectic things had been for her, and how distracted she was. The next time I saw her that week, she was in contention down the stretch, and she was standing over a 10-footer for birdie. She made the stroke, and her putterhead came through low and right down the target line. It was actually hitting the ground on that line as the ball was falling into the cup.

She just needed that one thing to focus on to help her clear out all the other distractions and mechanical thoughts that had been complicating her routine and her stroke. We didn't talk about setup. We didn't talk about whether or not the putter was open or closed at impact, or what shape her stroke was making or should make. She just needed to get back into her routine and feel the roll in her left hand, right down the target line.

# SIX

# The Mental Game

I'm sure you've seen the common element in most of what we've been talking about in the last five chapters: the importance of the mental game.

Of all the "instruction" I've ever gotten on putting, starting from my dad when I was just a kid, 90 percent of it has been on the mental side—maintaining my routine, staying positive, believing I would make every putt, and not blaming myself when the ball didn't go into the hole.

You're probably saying to yourself that it's easy to do all of those things when you're already a good putter.

Maybe.

But I would argue that if you spent 90 percent of your putting practice time on the mental side of putting (and the rest on the actual act of rolling the ball on the practice green), you'd get far more out of the effort than if you focused all that attention on the stroke itself.

It might not be "easy," but it's a quicker path to improvement than obsessing over mechanics.

Think for a second about something you do very well. It could be something at your job, or at home. Let's say it's woodworking. If you're a good woodworker, you have a place where you do the work, and you've got a set of tools to solve any situation that might come up. You're good at it, and you look forward to the chance to use your skills. The work itself comes "naturally," and you perform each part of the job without even thinking about it.

If you're good at doing anything, you obviously know how to do it. At some point, you got to a level where you trusted that you knew how to do it, and you let it go. What I'm trying to get you to see here is that you already know how to make the ball roll. You need to jump-start the development of your mental game to be able to get out of your own way.

For me, the basic skills to do that came from my dad and his determination to get me to concentrate on seeing the line and following my routine. But Dad was always on the lookout for other mental-side techniques he thought could help me when I went out on tour in 1966. One of those was a book called *Psycho-Cybernetics*, by Maxwell Maltz.

Maltz was a plastic surgeon who wanted to figure out why some of his patients weren't satisfied with the results of surgery—even when the surgery could be defined as a "success" in every sense of the word. They looked better, but they didn't feel better. His theory was that patients—or anybody else trying to improve at something—sabotaged themselves with negative self-talk.

That idea—along with a couple of others we'll talk about in a minute—made a lot of sense to me, so I highlighted it. Working my way through the book, I highlighted everything I liked, so that I could go back through my notes and catch the main points in about thirty minutes or so.

If you struggle with your putting, think about the way you approach every shot. When you hit a bad putt, what do you say to yourself? Golf is supposed to be fun—something most people do for enjoyment on a day off. But I work with hundreds of average players who call themselves the worst names when they hit a bad putt or make a bad read. They tell themselves they're terrible, or the worst putter of all time. They three-putt the first two holes and are convinced that they're never going to make another one the rest of the day.

And they're right.

Your brain is a powerful thing, and it is amazingly sensitive to suggestion. If you label yourself a bad putter and heap a bunch of negative self-talk on by the bucketful, you're going to be exactly what you call yourself.

That might sound discouraging and difficult to beat, but the solution is really straightforward.

In the same way that your brain is sensitive to negative self-talk, it's very receptive to *positive* talk, and to visualization.

One of the other key elements I picked up from *Psycho-Cybernetics* was the concept of seeing what you want to accomplish before you actually do it. You don't sit and hope you're successful, or think that all you want to do is knock it up there close and two-putt. You visualize exactly what's going to happen.

Going into the 1970 season, I had won four times in four seasons out on tour, but I was by no means patting myself on the back thinking I was set for life. I wasn't that great a ballstriker. I was still being referred to as the "unknown," or the "young Turk" in the newspapers. All I had was my mental abilities, a good short game, and the determination never to give up. When I first got out on tour, my sponsors got 80 percent and I got 20. I knew that if I won $400, I'd really only won $80. My dad had been recommending *Psycho-Cybernetics* for a while, and in the summer that season, I committed to pushing through and reading it. I wanted to do anything I could to improve, and to get sharper mentally.

At Southern Hills for the PGA Championship, I played my Monday practice round visualizing how the hill overlooking the 18th green would be filled with people rooting me on. I shot 66 in the third round to take a three-shot lead, and wouldn't you know it—when I walked up 18 on Sunday, that hill was filled with people. I ended up beating Arnold Palmer and Bob Murphy by two shots to win my first major championship.

One of the tools I took from the book was the idea of having a video of myself making a series of putts, from five feet all the way out to 50 feet. A company ended up creating one that looped over and over, with me making the putts with a great music score to go with it and the sound of the ball dropping into the bottom of the cup magnified. I was playing in the L.A. Open one year, and Cathy and I were staying with my friend Ron Rhoads, who was the head professional at Riviera Country Club (and was the best man at our wedding). I shot 73 the first day, with thirty-five putts, and I was steamed. Ron and Cathy knew I had the video, and they told me I needed to go watch it that night. Now, I wasn't in any mood to listen to advice from my "gallery," but I figured that watching it would at least get them to stop pestering me about it.

You can probably guess what happened next. I went out the next day and made everything—twenty-four putts for a 67, on a day when I hit it just terribly. Watching the video helped get me back in rhythm, and it made me mentally start seeing success and the ball going into the hole. It's absolutely magic. I was absorbing the feel and rhythm, the music was relaxing me, and it let me go out there and roll the ball without *trying* and getting tensed up.

The other great lesson I learned from the book was the idea that you need to know yourself and embrace who that is. I've never been a great ball-striker. But I have a great short game, and getting myself in position to use that short game was going to be my path to success. Starting with that PGA Championship at Southern Hills, my strategy was to play aggressively all the time. Wherever they put the flag on the green, I was going after it. If I short-sided myself and wound up in a tough spot, I was going to rely on my short game to bail me out. At Southern Hills, I finished 2-under for the tournament. I made twenty-two birdies, an eagle, twenty bogeys, and a double-bogey. On forty-five of the seventy-two holes, I was either cheering or groaning. I decided to take that risk, to live or die by my best skills.

The only place that strategy didn't work so well was at the U.S. Open. They set up those courses so that if you miss, even slightly, you can be in a place where a double-bogey is a good score. I used to get so frustrated and stressed out playing in those tournaments that I decided to use a completely different approach the week of the 1978 Open at Cherry Hills Country Club outside Denver—one you can adapt and use in your own pressure situation.

Instead of going in early and obsessively preparing like I would for other majors, I decided to treat that Open like it was the Colorado Open. It'd be nice to win a Colorado Open, but it wasn't going to change my career. It wasn't even like winning a tour event. So I never got to the course earlier than forty-five minutes before my tee time, and I never hit more than fifteen balls to warm up. After my rounds, I never did any practicing. I ended up one bad bounce away from winning the tournament. On the 18th hole, I hit a good tee shot down the right side of the fairway, and I don't know what it hit over there, but the ball kicked right, up the hill, and into deep grass. I made bogey there and lost to Andy North by a shot.

I realize it's not easy to flip a switch in your head so that you don't feel pressure. But pressure *is* 100 percent self-imposed. How you respond to it is partially physiological—the adrenaline starts pumping, or you start tensing up because of the stress of a certain situation. But you can short-circuit those kinds of physiological responses if you don't give yourself the chance to notice that you're actually *in* a pressure situation.

When Al Geiberger shot the first 59 in PGA Tour history in Memphis in 1977, I was playing with him and keeping his card. After every hole, Al's caddie would take his ball and put it in his pocket, and Al would ask for a fresh one on every tee. The caddie would take out the same ball and hand it to him, out of superstition. But Al was so much in the pressure-free zone of just hitting every shot as it came that he didn't even notice that it was the same ball. He went around all 18 holes with the same one, and broke the record.

For the average player, pressure is relative. You might feel pressure standing over a birdie putt. You might get tight when $10 is on the line with a friend, or when you're playing to win a match in a club tournament. Pressure comes from not having a game plan and a routine. The goal is to disconnect from the consequences of any putt and spend all of your energy on visualizing the putt going in, using the same process every time. Once you've done that, you've done all you can do.

One drill my son Ronnie likes to use is to push a tee into the ground two inches in front of the ball a player is about to roll. As the player makes the stroke, Ronnie asks him or her to give a snap assessment of the putt—good or not good—as the ball rolls over the tee. Doing that gets them focused on the process—which should be the same for every putt, regardless of the circumstances—rather than on making or missing. When players do this drill, they discover that they often struggle with the putter because they feel like they have to be absolutely perfect with their read and stroke for the ball to go in, when in fact that's not the case. They start to see that they can miss that tee by a little, or make a little less than perfect contact and not like the roll, and it still might go in.

Another way to disconnect from being so concerned about results is to stick some tees in the practice green and putt to those instead of to a hole. Can you roll the ball to the tee? All you're doing is seeing the line and rolling it, and getting into the mood where it's simple to you and there's no penalty phase when you miss one.

Even the best players struggle with pressure on the putting green. They might have a good routine, but when the heat is on, they go faster or slower, or they go from being talkative to being quiet. Everything you do differently than "normal" is just another signal to your brain and your body to tense up.

It's happened to me plenty of times, but never on a short-game shot. Long-game shots were always the weak link for me—the tee shot on 18 at Pebble Beach, or the fourth hole at Harbour Town. I overcame those stressful moments by getting a game plan and sticking to it, and getting clubs I trusted. I'm not trying to suggest that you'll be able to read this chapter and erase the emotions and nerves from your game forever. Nobody can do that. But even doing a *slightly* better job following your routine and forgetting about consequences will produce positive results in your putting.

When you start to tune in to your routine and your line, you won't have the time or the opportunity to watch what your playing partners' balls are doing as they roll by the hole. That might sound like a negative, but trust me, you're better off. I almost never watch another player in my group putt, for a couple of reasons. First, I don't know what his or her read was, or what he did with his stroke. If you watched me roll a 15-footer, I promise you couldn't tell from my stroke if I pulled it slightly, or if the ball went exactly where I planned. If my putt missed to the left because I pulled it, but you thought the read should have been more to the right, you're going to miss your putt to the right.

That's too much thinking for me.

I want to make my own read, see the line for myself, and concentrate on what I'm doing. I'll never forget playing with Jack Nicklaus for the first time, at the Canadian Open in 1966. I look at the yardage book and it says we've got 185 yards. The pin is back and a little downhill, so I figure it's about a 4-iron. But when I look down at Jack's bag, I see that he has his 3-iron out. I was nowhere near as long as Jack, so I'm thinking there's no way a 4-iron could be the right club for me. I pull out my 3, and proceed to knock it 15 yards over the green. We walk off the tee toward the green, and Jack says, "Don't look in my bag. You're not going to be able to tell if I'm hitting it full or 50 percent."

Lesson learned.

Another lesson you can take from Jack has to do with blame. Jack has had more important putts than anybody in the history of the game. Over forty years, he stood over hundreds of them. He certainly made far more than his share when they mattered most—but he didn't make all of them. But to hear Jack tell it, he never missed one when a tournament was on the line.

Jack isn't a liar. He's just the best kind of forgetful.

Good putters know that there's nothing to be gained by dwelling on the misses and blaming yourself for screwing something up. We're all human, and we all make mistakes, but it doesn't help to fill up your head with all those negative thoughts. There's value in keeping track of *why* a putt didn't do what you thought it would, either because of your speed control or your read, or something about your stroke. But you're only doing that kind of on-the-fly evaluation to improve your sense of feel on the next hole.

In other words, I don't care if you three-putt the first three holes. I want to hear self-talk at that point telling you that you're just about to go on your streak of one-putts, because you're due. Don't let the first twelve putts ruin your ability to make the next six. Most players who go through the rough stretch curse themselves out, call themselves every name they can think of, and resign themselves to what they just *know* is going to be a forty-putt day.

And thinking that way has just guaranteed that will happen.

Take pride in your routine, and enjoy the process. If you look at putting as something fun, and something to look forward to, you're immediately going to have more success. By immersing yourself in seeing the line and following your routine, you're taking an active role, versus being passive and reacting to what's happening. If you do happen to miss—and we all do, obviously—move on to the next putt, and approach it as if the previous one never happened. It's important not to blame yourself.

The ability to forget about the previous putt is definitely something of a trick you have to play on yourself. You can hear it in the press conferences the winning players give every week on the professional tours. The players who are in the positive zone are the ones who talk about rolling a fantastic putt that just didn't go in. They didn't miss it. Maybe a spike mark knocked it off line, or something else happened that was beyond their control. But they did what they wanted to do.

It's hard to stay in that positive, focused place for an extended period of time. I know that when I get toward the end of the season, I find myself watching more and more hunting shows on television, and wishing I was someplace other than the golf course. I know my mind isn't in the right place to play well—or putt well. And it almost always shows up in my results.

It's time to think about your own game, and why you're out there playing. I see so many people who tell me they play golf because they love the game, but they look absolutely miserable when they're on the putting green. You might not be able to keep that positive focus every single time you play, but try to start with one round—or even a few holes. I think you'll discover that calmer, simpler, more positive thinking will produce more positive results. Your game will feed off those feelings, and the results will come.

# SEVEN

# Why Equipment Matters, and When It Doesn't

The chapters on self-talk and equipment are next to each other in this book for a reason. Why? Because I bet the way you think about yourself and your putting game says a lot about the relationship you have with your putter.

When you learn feel and start to talk to yourself in a more positive, confident way, the piece of equipment you hold in your hand simultaneously starts to matter more and matter less.

Let me explain.

It starts to matter more because I believe that you can't be a good putter unless you treat your equipment with care and respect. It's like having a beautiful shotgun that just fits you, or a thirty-year-old fly rod that responds in your hands. Or a car that you absolutely love. You connect with all of those pieces of equipment, and it makes sense to treat them with respect and take care of them so you can use and enjoy them for a long time. You feel like the piece of equipment is going to *help* you do something well.

In that sense, the particular putter you use is an extremely personal choice, and it matters. I've used a variety of putters in my career, and if you leaned them against the wall in a line, you wouldn't see much of a common thread in terms of how they look. I won tournaments with a Wilson 8802 blade, a Ray Cook mallet, a Ping Anser 2, a Spalding HBA blade, and an Odyssey Rossi 2 mallet. (My favorite out of that group was the Ray Cook mallet. I won both of my PGAs with the exact same putter, one of two of that model I used off and on for almost thirty years.) A lot of the success I've had on the Champions Tour has come with something from TaylorMade's line of putters, usually either a mallet or a Daytona model. The one I use now is called the Ghost TM-110, and it has a black grooved face insert that really rolls the ball great.

They might not look alike, but when I picked every one of them to come into the game-day lineup, they all had the same quality. They felt good in my hands, and I liked the look of them when I put them down in front of me.

There are so many choices out there today—literally hundreds at any major off-course shop, lined up like firewood on the indoor practice green. You can have just about any kind of head shape, face material, weighting, and graphics you can imagine, and you can spend $25 or $250. Bobby Nichols won the 1964 PGA with a putter he bought out of a bin for $5. To an extent, though, you get what you pay for. Some of the newest technology, like the grooved face in the TaylorMade Ghost series, really helps you. They're easy to align, the grooved face puts a great roll on the ball, and the white color cuts glare.

When I ask the players who come to one of my schools or clinics how they picked the putter they use, some of the answers fascinate me. Some players say they got the "name" putter they use as a prize at a tournament, or as a gift. Other players say they watched a friend make everything one day with the same model, so they went out and got the same one.

Other players try to be more "scientific" about it. They peg themselves as an arc putter, or as a straight-back-straight-through player, so they went out and got a putter that supposedly fit their kind of stroke.

I don't have any problem with any of those methods, as long as the result is what I would call a "feel fit." But, unfortunately, if that "feel fit" happens under those circumstances, it's because of luck—like picking up a random set of keys at the valet stand and hoping you end up with a car you like. You might get some clues from the logo on the keys (or the putter), but you need to take a test drive before you make your decision.

When you guide your putter selection by how the club feels in your hand, how it looks when you put it down in front of you, how it fits you physically, and how the ball feels when you roll it, you're going to end up with something that inspires more confidence. I believe that "match" has more to do with how pleasing the head shape is to your eye, the loft on the face and the kind of grip on the club than any specific "style" the club has.

In that sense, the *particular* kind of putter you have in your hand matters less, as long as it feels good to you and helps you.

Now, do I believe that the average player can benefit from new putter technology? Absolutely. The new putters dramatically reduce the penalty for missing the sweet spot on the face, and the material and groove technology improve the quality of the roll for anybody, regardless of their skill level.

But what I'm trying to get across is that it's not as easy as pulling one of the new white TaylorMade Ghost putters off the rack and heading out. Putting is an art, and the relationship you have (or should have) with your putter is an emotional one.

Let's talk about how to build that bond.

The most basic element is a physical fit. Andy North is a tall guy, but he bent way over and choked down on the putter. Both Ray Floyd and Steve Stricker stand tall and closer to the ball. The length of the shaft and lie angle of the putter—the angle between the sole and the shaft—have to suit your body and your posture. If you have shorter arms, you're probably going to use a longer putter with a flatter lie angle. If you have longer arms, your putter will probably be shorter and more upright. The vast majority of players will use a club between 33 and 35 inches long, with a lie angle between 69 and 73 degrees. You need to go to a shop with a wide variety of putters of different lengths and lofts and sort through to find the ones that feel comfortable at setup—regardless of head shape. I'll bet that when you give them to the fitter to be measured, they'll have similar lengths and lie angles.

Going back to that line of putters I used to win tournaments over a forty-year span, they don't look the same, but they do have a lot in common. They're all between 34 and 35 inches long, depending on head shape. They all have the same lie angle, and the same loft on the face. They all have the same style of grip, too. Ben Crenshaw and I used the same Golf Pride model with a flat top. I actually shaved both sides of the grip down a little because I liked the way it made the back of the grip feel rounded. The grip I use now is TaylorMade's version of that one, with a flat top, rounded back, and thin sides.

But by far the two biggest characteristics they share are loft and balance. I always want to be able to look down when I'm at address and see the face. We've talked about how important the forward press is in the stroke—and starting out with 4 degrees of loft on the face of the putter lets you forward

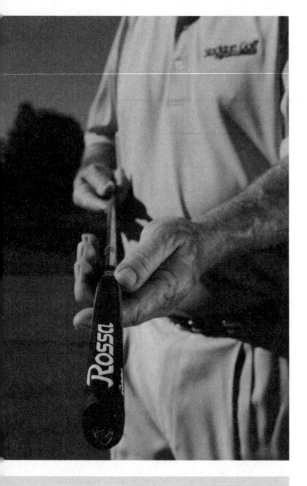

I prefer to use a putting grip with a flat top, which gives you a clear indicator of where the thumbs should rest on the handle.

press and keep loft on the face through impact for a good roll. When a putter has little or no loft, it causes you to subconsciously shift the grip back, away from the hole, to see more of the face. It's hard to roll the ball well from there. We've given lessons where the player comes in with a putter with two degrees of loft on their putter, and when they forward press, they hit the ball with the top edge of the blade and the ball shoots off to the right. You want to make sure you have enough loft on the putterface so that there's some loft of the face at impact.

As far as balance goes, I think it's important for a putter to feel "light" in your hands. I don't want to pick it up and immediately feel the weight of the clubhead. Some players go with a heavier head because they think it helps keep them steadier, or because they feel that they don't have to make as big a swing. I think that's robbing yourself of a lot of the sensitivity in your fingers. I want a balanced putter, not a heavy head or a heavy grip. When I played the regular tour, I would occasionally switch to a heavier putter to contend with slow greens, like the ones at the British Open. But when I added weight to the clubhead, I'd add similar weight in the form of lead tape under the grip, so that the actual swing weight of the putter wasn't much different from my standard gamer.

If you struggle with your stroke, you'd probably be better off with a putter that's face-balanced. Face-balanced weighting means the putter wants to stay square through impact. That gives you a larger sweet spot across the face, for when you don't catch the ball right in the center. To check if a putter is face-balanced, balance the shaft on your finger, up near the head. If the face is horizontal and parallel to the ground, the putter is face-balanced.

The style and material of the grip you use is definitely a matter of preference, but I want to make a couple of overall points about how your choice can affect your stroke. The style and size of grip you use should absolutely feel good to you, but you have to be careful not to use a grip that is too small. If the grip is small in your fingers, your tendency is to hold on tighter with your fingers to stabilize it. That tension is not good for feel.

As far as larger-diameter grips go, I had always believed that the increased size also produced tension, but my opinion on that has changed. When I started working with Massy Kuramoto, he was using a putter with a fat grip on it. Honestly, I teased him a little bit about it, to the point that he switched it back to a conventional-size grip. But the next week, I saw Mark Johnson using the same grip, and he handed me the club to try. I rolled in twelve putts in a row. I didn't like the feel as much as I do my own grips, but I didn't feel any extra tension in my hands. As long as the size doesn't get out of control, and doesn't change the overall balance of the putter, I think it's an option to consider.

And really, the only way to narrow it down and find the putter for you is to try a bunch. You can get some insight into what putters are popular by checking a tour player's bag, especially if he or she is using a different brand of putter than the rest of the clubs in the bag. Tour players don't mess around with putters. If it works, they're putting it in the bag, regardless of the brand. The models that are popular on tour are a good starting point, but putter companies make a wide variety of clubs within the same line for a reason. You can get the new TaylorMade Ghost model in a dozen different head shapes and a wide variety of graphics. I picked the Ghost TM-110 model because it has a simple look, the white finish really cuts down on glare and stands out against the green grass, and the black True Roll insert makes it easy for me to see the face and create a fantastic roll.

The graphics on the top of the putter are a matter of taste, but they also serve an important purpose. The lines are there to help you line up the putter square to the target line. Some players like to see a lot of lines—two set the same width as the ball with another one in the middle is a common configuration—while other players like to see one single aiming line in the middle of the top of the head. It used to be that the line on the top of the head signified where the sweet spot was on the face—the place where the ball came off with the truest roll. The new materials they're using in the face inserts and the quality of the groove and weighting technology mean that you can miss the "sweet spot" slightly and still get a good roll. The grooves on the face of the TaylorMade model I use are designed to get the ball rolling sooner without much skidding right after impact, which can happen with smooth-faced putters. The grooves are as important on a putter as a wedge. You wouldn't want to try to control a shot with a wedge that had no grooves—but that's a discussion for another book. I feel like I don't have to be perfect in terms of hitting the sweet spot, and I'm still going to have control over the speed and roll. I'm more concerned about stroking it through impact with a square face and starting the ball on my line.

You can adjust the actual physical feel you get when the ball and putterface meet in several different ways. The kind of ball you use is a big factor. "Game improvement" balls designed for low spin and more distance have a harder feel, while the tour-level balls like the TaylorMade Penta have a softer cover for more feel and spin around the green. The face inserts (or the faces themselves) also are made from different materials and have a variety of hardness levels. Your goal is to match the ball and face material with the feel you like. You might like a soft, muted sound at impact, or you might like a firmer "click."

Once you've settled on your "gamer," you're almost done, but not quite. I think it's good to have two or three different-style putters with the same basic length-loft-lie configuration. If you start feeling less confident with your gamer, you can switch to one of the backups to get a different look. I've switched in and out of blade putters, mallets, and perimeter-weighted putters. And regardless of what the actual measurements are on a putter, trust your eye. You could give me a scientific certification showing 4 degrees of loft on the face of a Bullseye putter, and I'd still want to flip it around and use it left-handed because it just doesn't look like the face has any loft to me. And no matter how the ball actually comes off the face, if you don't feel good looking at the head—either because you have trouble aligning the face, or it just looks plain ugly to you—try something else.

When it comes to experimenting, some players who don't see any success with one of the alternative grips we talked about, like the cross-handed or the saw, take the next step and try a belly or a long putter.

With a long putter, the concept is pretty simple. You hold the top handle of the long shaft in your left hand and anchor your hand to the center of the chest. The right hand goes on the lower handle and provides the power for the stroke. Honestly, I don't know how anchoring the club on your chest can be considered a legal stroke, but the USGA says it's OK. With a belly putter, your hands hold onto the handle normally, but the extended grip is anchored in your belly.

If you have a serious case of the yips or a bad back that keeps you from bending over much, I can see how a long putter could help you, but I'd never put you in a long putter if I could possibly avoid it. J. B. Holmes came to see me for a lesson, and his luggage didn't arrive with his flight. While we waited, he hit some putts with my putter, incorporating the techniques we've been talking about over the last few chapters. Twenty minutes later, he was blown away by how different he felt rolling the ball. He threw out the long putter and went back to a standard-length one. I just believe that feel is in the hands. When I was helping Bernhard Langer a bit, he let me try his long putter, and it was like using a javelin. But some guys seem to be able to do pretty well with it. Bruce Lietzke is the best I've ever seen with the long putter in his hand. My son Dave Jr. works with Martin Laird on tour now, and Martin really rolls it great with one, too.

If you're determined to go with the longer club, find one with the right shaft length—the top of the handle should hit right on your solar plexus—and make sure the lie angle is right. You're going to be more upright than you would be with a conventional putter, but you still want your ball position to be under your eyes, like it would be with a normal putter. If the club is too upright, the ball will be too close to you, and vice versa. It's also important to remember that you don't forward press with a long putter, so you don't need more than about two degrees of loft on the face.

Technique-wise, you need to keep your weight on your front leg so you can avoid hanging back and hitting up on the putt. You also aren't going to be able to incorporate a forward press for a smooth, dynamic start to the stroke, so it's important not to spend too much time frozen over the ball after you step into your stance.

The last piece of advice I have for you on equipment might sound

I keep my putter in the top divider, headcover on, with my driver, woods, and hybrids—all taller clubs with headcovers. That way, I know it won't get knocked around and beat up by the shorter irons.

unimportant, but it's an important step to becoming a real player. As I said at the beginning of the chapter, you can't be a good putter unless you treat your equipment with respect. Put your putter in the top end of the bag, with your driver and other woods, and keep the headcover on it. Don't stick it in the bottom divider of your bag along with your wedges, where it can get beat to all hell. If it bangs around with the other short clubs, it can get nicks and dings on the face and leading edge. Those bumps and bruises are distracting, and they can cause the face to shine, which makes it hard to see.

Once you make the commitment to take care of your putter, keep up with the maintenance, too. Most players understand that they need to change the grips on their irons and woods, but they keep the grip on their putter for way too long. You don't put the same kind of wear on a putting grip as you do on a club you use for full swings, but you hold your putter in your hands for way more time during a round than any other club. The sweat and dirt on your hands breaks down the putting grip over time and makes it slick. When the grip loses that tackiness, you tend to subconsciously hold it a little tighter—producing tension. Spend the five or ten bucks for a fresh one every six months, at least.

It's worth it.

# EIGHT

# Troubleshooting

You've gone through seven chapters now, and I hope you've come to two main conclusions. The first is that I believe that the mental side of putting is far more important than the mechanical side. The second is that the fundamental challenge in putting is to absorb advice—whether it's about a routine, seeing the line, or even how to hold the putter—enough to use it effectively, but to not get paralyzed by analysis. There comes a point when you have to decide that you know it, and get on to using it and feeling it.

A major part of that process is developing a straightforward sense of personal feedback. Remember that we're not concerned about results in terms of making putts or missing them. The goal is to see the line and roll the putt on the line you picked. As you roll each putt and play each hole, you want to be able to accumulate information about what your ball is doing so that you can make adjustments if necessary—either during the round, or in a post-round practice session.

Before I get into how to go through that process, I want to describe for you what my practice, pre-round, and post-round routines are, to reinforce the idea that putting well isn't about crouching over four hundred repetitions of the same putt and obsessing about mechanics. Everything I do—and everything you should be doing—revolves around fine-tuning the feel in my hands and fingers and getting a sense for what the particular green conditions are that day.

Players and students always ask me how much time I spend practicing putting when I'm away from a tournament site or in the off-season. The answer—both forty-five years ago and today—is virtually none. As I'm getting ready to start a season, or play a tournament after a long layoff, I might go out and roll a few putts to check out a new putter model that TaylorMade has sent me, or to see how good my back feels, but I'm not out there grinding away to make sure a body part is in perfect position.

If you're determined to go out and practice your putting, I want you to focus your effort on the quality of the practice and the information you get from seeing your line and rolling your ball, not on monotonous repetition. With that in mind, you should never practice with more than two balls at a time, and you need to change up the length and break of the putts you're practicing after every sequence of two putts. Why? Because rolling the same putt time after time and copying the same line doesn't do anything to improve your ability to read a putt, or your visualization of the line. Roll two 10-footers with slight right-to-left break, then switch to 20-footers with a big left-to-right curve. Change it around constantly, so that you're always exercising your reading, visualization, and speed-control skills.

Your constant goal in practice should be to go through your full routine before every putt, so that every one feels like it has the same consequences— see the line, roll the ball, and end up no more than 16 inches past the hole. You'll be shocked at just how much your abilities at all three of those skills will improve simply by adding that variety to your practice routine.

A "practice session" is by definition different from a "warm-up" or a "pre-round" session. Much like with the full swing, practice sessions are for working on your game, while warm-ups are for getting yourself into the playing mind-set and gathering information about the playing conditions you'll face.

Before a tournament round, I'm walking around the practice green finding putts that represent the ones I'm going to see out on the course. If your home course has super-undulating greens, you need to use the same two-ball strategy we just talked about for practice time and hit a variety of breaking putts. Making them is not as important as registering the green speed and firmness in your mental computer. At Augusta, most of my pre-tournament practicing was from downhill positions, because the greens always get faster as the week progresses.

The more information you can feed into the system, the better your subconscious mind will process it during the round itself. Rolling some putts on a brittle, burned-out, firm practice green will get you mentally prepared for some challenging putts on the course. It will also remind you that you can only control your own part of the equation. Follow your routine, see your line, and roll your ball. If bumps or aeration holes knock it off line, that's bad luck, not poor skill.

We've spent a lot of time talking about how important positive self-talk is, so it shouldn't surprise you that I'm a big fan of setting yourself up with some good feelings before you walk off the practice green to the first tee. I always go to the practice green eleven or twelve minutes before my tee time and spend the first eight minutes rolling the ball on various contours to get my feel. In that last bit of time, I move closer to the hole and roll some short putts in from various angles. Seeing and hearing the ball go into the hole is a subconscious positive, and it gives you a clean, calm transition from preparation time to competition time.

It used to be that three hours was a slow time for walking 18 holes and carrying your own bag. Now, even with carts, public-course players are looking at four-and-a-half or even five-hour rounds. With the game taking so long now, asking you to spend fifteen or twenty minutes on the practice green after you play is a stretch. But if you want to get the most out of your practice time, try to carve out some post-round time at least every second or third time you play. It's some of the most valuable practice time you have.

I like to go and roll some putts after I play because I've just spent a lot of time out on the course—in the real world, so to speak. If I consistently missed putts on a certain side of the hole, that fact is going to be fresh in my mind right after the round, and I can make some adjustments in practice to feel better about my day. There's a big difference between the fresh memory of some mistakes you made on the course and the simple, raw number on the scorecard itself. Even if you track your putts on the card, the number thirty-five or forty is just that—a number—once you've cracked open your first beer at the 19th hole. It might represent a "bad" putting round, but the general "bad" tag doesn't help you attack the real part of your putting game that needs the attention.

Identifying your specific kind of miss is a huge first step toward getting better. The next step is to understand *why* the ball didn't roll on the correct line. As we've been talking about repeatedly, it starts with routine. Phil Mickelson's old routine—a series of short looks at the hole—prevented him from seeing the line as well as he could, and from translating his original look at the line to an actual roll. By simplifying his routine, he started putting better—independent of anything having to do with his stroke.

You might be thinking to yourself that your routine is pretty consistent. I have to say that I've seen very few that are good—pro or amateur. Most of them have extra steps, or they change depending on the situation, or depending on the pressure of the putt at hand. Remember, you want to identify your own putting signature and use a routine that gives you the best chance to sign that signature on the putt. As I write this, Martin Laird and Sandra Gal won tournaments on the PGA Tour and LPGA Tour by making putts on the 18th hole without any practice stroke. Martin two-putted from 87 feet, and his four-footer for the win never had a chance to miss. Both of their routines stayed at the same speed, as if they were making any other putt.

Before we get to missing putts left or right—which could have to do with the quality of the read or the direction of the stroke—are you rolling the putt the right distance? Distance is far more important than direction. Do you consistently leave yourself awkward comeback putts? Do you usually leave putts short, or hit them too far by the hole? Do you feel like your speed control is inconsistent? Isolating a speed problem—versus a read problem—helps narrow your focus and gives you something to address as far as drills or training aids go.

If speed is the problem, you can attack it several ways. First, make sure you're rolling the ball. Check the loft on your putter. Many, many students come to me with the problem of flipping their hands at the ball, or hitting at it instead of rolling the putt, strictly because they're using a putter with no loft. By using a putter with loft, and starting your stroke with a forward press, you immediately change the dynamics of contact with the ball. It becomes much easier to put a consistent roll on the ball, and you become much more sensitive to distance. You give yourself back the feel you already have in your fingers.

With the routine, seeing the line, and developing a feel for speed, you're adding to the consistency of your stroke piece by piece. Even during practice, you need to keep your self-talk positive, and not worry about making the putt or missing it. You're going to follow your routine, let it go, and roll the ball over your spot in front of the ball. If you can do it consistently during practice, you're building a habit that becomes second nature. The goal is to go through the same routine on a practice putt as you would for par on the third hole or birdie on the 17th.

As I've said, I'm not interested in giving you a bunch of mechanical moves to copy. But if you've established that your routine is good and you have some control over the speed of the putt, how do you analyze what happens when you have poor direction? First, you differentiate between the quality of the read and a mistake in your stroke. With experience, that gets easier and easier. I know when I've rolled the putt exactly the way I want. If the putt has a tricky break and the ball ends up moving more or less than I expected, I can live with that. It's when you miss because of a stroke mistake that you need to pay attention, so you can make a change.

It's important to understand why the distinction is so important. Many players make a bad read, or hit a putt too hard, and it goes into the hole because the poor speed compensated for the bad read. In other words, where I see a 10-footer that will enter the hole at four o'clock, the bad putter played the putt as if it was 13 feet long and rammed it straight in—or read it as having too much right-to-left break and then pulled it. Understanding the difference between making a good stroke and missing the right line and making a bad stroke and lucking it into the hole will by itself dramatically improve your ability to read greens. Why? Because when you miss, you'll know why you missed, and you'll make a better adjustment for the next putt. As those adjustments build on top of each other in your subconscious, you're improving your overall feel and skill. That's so much better than a "hit and hope" philosophy, don't you think?

If I know I missed because of a poor stroke, the roll of the ball tells me what I need to know about fixing it. When you miss a putt to the left, it's probably because the ball was too far away from you and you lowered your hands. That causes the putter to move on more of an exaggerated arc, and it's easier to close the face or pull it. Players have the common bad habit of allowing the toe of the putter to lift up in the air at address, and I believe it comes from letting full-swing setup fundamentals creep into the putting game. Your putter is built on more of an upright lie angle than your irons or your driver, and you need to be closer to the ball with it. When you set up to a putt like you're hitting a 7-iron, you're going to be too far away, and your hands will have to move lower to compensate.

In truth, misses to the left are much easier to account for and correct than misses to the right. Most poor putters make poor contact and miss right—almost like they'd slice a full shot. If you're using a putter that doesn't have enough loft, you're going to hang back and flip the right hand through impact, which will more often than not cause the putter to come through open and high. You'll also make weak contact high on the ball if you have a tendency to lift your head or your left shoulder through the stroke to see where the ball is going. We're going to talk about a couple of drills shortly that will help fight that tendency.

I hesitate to use such mechanical terminology here, because I don't want you to lose the main point. I'm not trying to give you a "tip," or a Band-Aid for your putting stroke. For you to be a good putter, you need to understand what your ball is doing and adapt your stroke in a natural way to account for any problems that are creeping in. If I start missing putts to the right consistently, I don't think about the exact mechanics of what I'm doing or not doing. I simply take the putter back heel first. If I miss it left consistently, I lift my hands slightly away from my body and possibly stand a little closer to the ball. It's like turning the hot and cold knobs in the shower to get the right temperature. The temperature that feels good might change a little from day to day, and you make slight adjustments to the hot or cold knob to get the right mix. You don't read a piece of paper that says, "Turn hot knob three inches. Turn cold knob two inches."

In my case, if the ball is missing left, I know great putting is about to start with those minor adjustments. Both Kenny Perry at the 2008 Ryder Cup and Rory McIlroy after the 2011 Masters found out how quickly left misses can be cured. In Kenny's case, we talked about it briefly in a practice round before the event, and it led to one of the greatest putting rounds in history. With Rory, it took five minutes for him to see that adjusting his hands just a little higher made them go in.

We're not machines, and we're never going to be perfect. All we can do is be as tuned in as possible to how we feel that day. I believe I've been a great putter my entire career because I never considered myself a work in progress. Once I had my routine down, I believed I could do it. Whether it was true or not didn't matter. I believed it was, so I didn't worry about results or minute little adjustments or mechanical thoughts. I didn't lose sleep trying to be perfect.

Looking back, I think my dad was a genius at setting me up with that confidence. The basics he taught me, and the simple drills we used when I was a kid, built that foundation. I learned how to see the line and to roll the ball, but without getting bogged down in endless mechanical thoughts.

Honestly, it's tougher to peel away all the layers of overanalysis and mechanical crud that have built up over the years than it is to start fresh, but you'll be amazed at how quickly you can simplify your routine and your stroke by trying these few drills. They're really going to help your feel. I don't think you need to go out and buy a trunk full of training aids to putt well, either. You basically need some guides to help judge your results and dial in your alignment and aim. We use the Stockton Golf Rings at our clinics—a set of thin folding rings that go down on the green to provide a circular target area. They're easy to see, and the ball rolls over them without getting caught up. Another valuable tool is a simple carpenter's chalk line. It snaps down on the grass to create a temporary guideline. You can get one for $5 from the hardware store. Use one on the practice green to mark off a straight 10-footer, then use the chalk line to line up the aiming line on your putter. Now you know the face is lined up square to where you want the ball to go. You're equating what you see as straight with what actually is straight. That's something that can get knocked out of whack from time to time.

## DAD'S GRIP DRILL

Instead of telling me what all my various body parts should be doing during a stroke, my dad taught me how to putt by emphasizing what the putter should do. He wanted me to keep the putter low to the ground through the stroke and let my left hand be dominant. Everything else was just window-dressing. So instead of telling me how to stand or what my stroke shape should be, he simply stood alongside my line holding the butt of a club about three inches in front of the back of my left hand at address. My only mission was to make a stroke and hit the end of my dad's club flush with the back of my left hand. Doing that was more important than where the ball ended up, or anything else. This drill accomplished a lot of important things. First, it simplified the stroke, so I was thinking about one simple thing—not what my elbows were doing, or if my stroke was a perfect arc, or if my shoulders

This drill is one of the first ones my dad ever used with me, and I've passed it on to my sons—and my students. Set up to a putt and have a friend stand in front of you, holding another club so that the grip is about three inches from the back of your left hand (1). When you roll the putt, keep the putter low to the ground through the stroke and push the back of your left hand into the grip your friend is holding (2). If you let the left wrist lift or break down and flip (3), you'll miss the guide club completely.

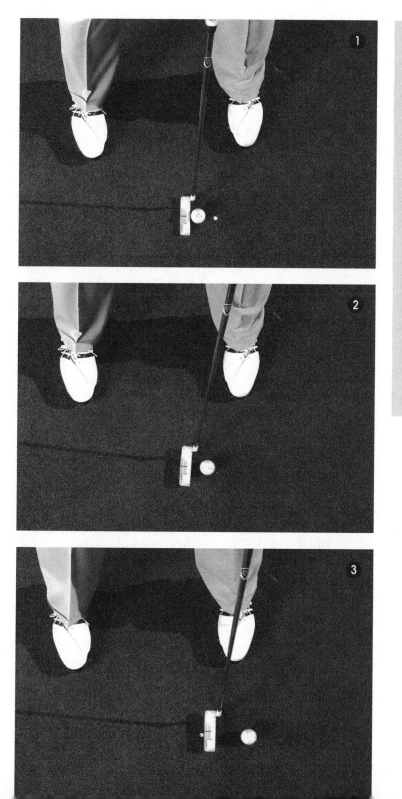

When I choose my line, I identify a spot an inch or so in front of my ball on that line (1) and make it my goal to roll my ball over that line. If I've done that (2), and use good speed, I've done my job. I want the putter to stay low to the ground through impact, so I keep my focus on the spot, on the first four or six inches of my line (3), until the ball is long gone.

were set at the right angle. If I could hit the club with the back of my left hand, it meant that I was keeping the putter low and putting a good roll on the ball. To do it, it meant that I was keeping my head still and down, and that I wasn't flipping my hands through impact—all subconscious stroke improvements that came from simply concentrating on one task. Even to this day, doing this drill with one of my sons helps clear my mind of anything other than simply rolling the ball.

## CROSS THE TEE

Another simple visualization technique my dad used with me was to push a tee into the ground an inch or so in front of my ball, on the line I was about to putt. My goal was to go through my routine, see my line, set up to the ball looking at my target, use my last glance down to look at the tee, and then roll the ball over that tee. Focusing on a closer target helps keep you from being so concerned about results. You want to feel like you're making a good roll, and once you do that, the make or miss is out of your control. My son Ron uses this drill extensively with pros and amateurs. He asks them to roll the ball over the tee and judge the stroke before the ball even gets to the target. He asks them to say "yes" or "no" about the roll before the ball has even gone a foot. It helps disconnect the idea of consequences—using the same routine for every stroke is the goal—and helps them see that you don't have to be perfect for the ball to go into the hole.

## NARROWING YOUR FOCUS, EXPANDING THE HOLE

Being able to see the line and roll the ball on that line incorporates two read elements: speed and break. When I make my read, I'm picking a very specific spot where I see the ball falling into the hole, and I'm planning to roll the ball no more than 18 inches past the hole if I miss. Practicing with some visual aids is a great way to help assess how well you're accomplishing those two goals.

Find a 12- or 15-foot putt on the practice green that has an appreciable break to it. Go through your routine and see your line, but before you get into

your stance, go over and stick a tee into the edge of the cup where you see the ball entering the hole. Now go back and go through your entire routine again, but go ahead and roll the putt. Your goal, obviously, is to bounce the ball gently off the tee at the spot where it should fall into the cup. This part of the drill also helps you see that rolling the ball with touch and speed so that it dies into the cup— and reading enough break into the putt—is a benefit. Play the ball a little too high, but with good speed, and it

Two critical parts of seeing the line are picking the point at which the ball will enter the hole and rolling the ball with the ideal speed. Pick a 12-foot putt with some break—six inches or so—and place a tee in the edge of the hole where you want the ball to enter. Practice rolling putts so that they bounce off that tee (1). If you play too little break, the ball has little chance to go in. Play the ball a little high, but with good speed, and it can still drop into the hole. To work on speed, place a 20-inch Stockton Golf Ring around the front edge of hole and practice rolling puts so that if they miss, they don't go beyond the edge of the ring, 16 inches past the hole (2).

can trickle into the hole above the tee. Play it too low and you have little chance to make it.

The second part of this drill—you can do it together with the tee in the cup, at the same time—has to do with judging speed. With the 20-inch Stockton Golf Ring, you can make a circle around the hole, and practice rolling the ball to the tee in the edge of the cup. If you miss, the ball should still stay inside the ring, which means you've kept it within 16 inches. I don't like to leave putts short, so the "positive" area would be from the hole itself to the edge of the ring 16 inches past.

## LEFT-HAND DOMINANCE

As we've discussed, I believe that the left hand should dominate the stroke as the direction hand. If the right hand—which is the feel hand—does too much, you can end up hitting or popping the ball through impact, and you're making more of a strike than a roll. A hit is harder to control, and it makes it a lot harder—if not impossible—to judge speed. This drill goes hand-in-hand (so to speak) with the first one I described, hitting the back of the left hand on the handle of the second club. This time, make a series of strokes holding the putter with just your left hand. You'll quickly notice that the best way to make a controlled stroke is to let the clubhead swing and stay low to the ground. You can't produce any kind of decent roll flipping your hand or jerking on the grip end of the club. Make some strokes holding your left shoulder with your right hand—to encourage your shoulders to stay level—and start with the forward press you'd use in a regular stroke. It should feel like your left hand is moving right down the target line. If you don't feel like you have enough control over the club with the one hand, choke down on the grip slightly and let the handle rest against the flat of your wrist. One of my basic checks is to make sure the handle is still vertical at the end of the stroke, and not pointed back at my belly button.

These drills are designed to let you get out of your own way and concentrate on the line and feel. You want to get to the point where you're totally concentrating on where you want the ball to go, not on how you're going to

Practice making strokes with just the left hand (1), to get the feeling of the left hand dominating and the putter staying low to the ground. You can hold your left shoulder with your right hand (2) to encourage the left shoulder to stay level and not lift through the stroke. Let the putter swing through smoothly and stay low to the ground, instead of flipping your hand at the ball (3).

physically make it go there. Once you're there—and it'll happen—you'll truly be putting unconsciously.

I was out on the practice green the other day, working with a couple of tour players, when Sean O'Hair came over to talk. He wasn't looking for any help—he just wanted to watch me roll a couple of putts. The first thing he said afterward didn't have anything to do with my mechanics. He said it was incredible how relaxed I was, and how effortless it looked.

That's a big part of what I want for you, and what I hope you get from this book. It's not about making a perfect mechanical stroke, or *being* perfect. In 1972, I went more than 950 holes without a three-putt. I got to the U.S. Open at Pebble Beach and I had 10 three-putts and a four-putt, and I was on my way home after two rounds. You're not going to make them all.

The key ideas are simple. Find your own signature and stick to it, and follow a consistent routine. Feel it instead of trying to do it. Improve your visual interpretation of the speed and line of your putt, and roll the ball without wasting too much time and letting that visualization deteriorate.

If you can do those things, you're going to be more relaxed, more effortless, and more *unconscious*. You're going to enjoy yourself more (and play a round in less than five hours, which is a nice side benefit).

You're going to know exactly where to go, and you're going to use this book to get there.

Thanks for spending some time with me, and good luck.

## ACKNOWLEDGMENTS

While growing up on the south side of Arrowhead Country Club in San Bernardino with my parents, Audrey and Gail Stockton, I started a process that would lead me to USC and, upon graduation, a career spanning forty-six-plus years on the PGA Tour.

The game of golf became my life.

For forty-six years, my wife, Catherine, has been a very special partner and my best friend, and together we've formed a very unique team. With the addition of Dave Jr. in 1968 and Ronald in 1970, we slowly created a family business. Dave Jr. played the PGA Tour for more than nine years, and he's been teaching for the last two. Ron has been a teacher for more than twenty years, and he's taught me for more than twenty-five—ever since my father passed away.

As I was organizing my thoughts for this book, I was fortunate enough to be inducted into the Southern California Golf Association Hall of Fame. At the ceremony, my good friend Tom Self introduced me, and he told an amazing story about my dad's background in the game—a story I had never heard. Alex Morrison was one of the most prominent teachers in the 1930s and 1940s. He taught Henry Picard—who would go on to win the Masters in 1938 and the 1939 PGA Championship, and later work with Ben Hogan and Sam Snead—and he wrote a popular instruction book called *Better Golf Without Practice,* which came out in 1940. It turns out that Morrison taught my dad, and many of the mental principles Dad passed on to me came from Morrison all those years ago.

I had never thought to ask Dad where his knowledge came from. I just did what he told me. It was a special, special treat to discover more details about my father in this process, and to page through Morrison's book and see some of those familiar words and ideas.

My dad gave me a priceless foundation in the game and in life. Thanks to him, I was able to go out on the PGA Tour with confidence and a mental routine that would stay with me for more than forty years of competition. I use what he taught me every day, and it's the heart of what I share here.

From my college years at USC, I made so many close friends—especially Al Geiberger, who I followed through Kappa Alpha fraternity to become a PGA Champion, just as he did. Donna Caponi-Byrnes became the sister I never had, and we've taught each other throughout the years. Cathy and I met Jim and Lou Langley when we first went out on tour, and that was the start of a long friendship. Jim was the head professional at Cypress Point for more than thirty years and is a trusted set of eyes. Laurie and Marlene Hammer are great friends and great teammates. We won the Haig & Haig Mixed Scotch Foursome at La Costa together in 1967. And I owe a debt of gratitude to many fellow pros who offered tips throughout the years, including Don January, Byron Nelson, Lee Trevino, Dale Douglass, Jack Nicklaus, Dow Finsterwald, Gary Player, Arnold Palmer, Paul Azinger, and Phil Mickelson—among so many others.

I want to give thanks to the PGA of America, an organization I've been proud to be a part of for more than forty years, for selecting me as the Ryder Cup Captain in 1991 at Kiawah Island. Cathy and I spent a year and half promoting that special event, and it was an incredible thing to play a part in that great victory. That week was also the first sighting of the expanded Team Stockton. Dave Jr. and Ron were my only two assistants that week. To be an assistant captain for Paul Azinger seventeen years later for the Ryder Cup victory at Valhalla was another great thrill.

Special thanks must go to my agent, Ralph Cross, who has been a guiding influence throughout my career. Ralph is a trusted advisor and a good friend, and this book would not have been possible without him. It was great to work with Matt Rudy on the words, and I'm looking forward to all the *Golf Digest* articles we're going to be doing together. J. D. Cuban did a great job on both the photographs for the book and the videos you can see on Dave Stockton.com. Scott Waxman and Farley Chase got us a great deal with Gotham, where we were in good hands with Travers Johnson.

I feel blessed to have come full circle—to be able to pass my dad's ideas on to my boys, and to finish my career as a teacher. It's proving to be much more satisfying than playing for individual results. Now, with the boys and I working together full-time, teaching, we're going on seventy-plus years of Stockton family golf.

I'm very proud of that.